COLUMBUS
UNCOVERED

D1570516

COLUMBUS
UNCOVERED

Fascinating, Real-Life Stories About
Unusual People, Places & Things in
Ohio's Capital City

JOHN M. CLARK

Columbus, Ohio

Columbus Uncovered: Fascinating, Real-Life Stories About Unusual

People, Places & Things in Ohio's Capital City

Published by Gatekeeper Press

2167 Stringtown Rd, Suite 109

Columbus, OH 43123-2989

www.GatekeeperPress.com

ISBN (paperback): 9781619845664

eISBN: 9781642376784

Printed in the United States of America

For Jan, without whom this book would never have been finished. I love you. And for little Ruby Clark, who kept me company through much of the work. Yes, I love you, too.

TABLE OF CONTENTS

ACKNOWLEDGMENTS

Jan Clark
Ruby Rawls Clark
Jane Yokley
Cindy Hurt
Andy Marfurt
Doug Motz
Clark Grave Vault Company
Steve Skilken
Steve Wagner
Brent Turner
Krema Nut Company
James Fifield
Andrew Livelsberger
Columbus Metropolitan Library
Judith Steele
Dave Fisher
Jason, Claire, Al & the Entire Staff at Stauf's German Village

INTRODUCTION

THE BOOK YOU'RE holding came about because of my fascination for strange places, peculiar people and oddball events. Every city has them, and my adopted hometown of Columbus, Ohio, is no exception. There's the scheming entrepreneur whose fake elixir led to the creation of the Food and Drug Administration. Charles Lindbergh's efforts to put the city at the forefront of an air travel revolution. Frank Lloyd Wright's unusual advice to a local couple. The list goes on and on.

Each presented itself to me as a hint or a rumor or an old photo that, with enough sleuthing, developed into one of the dozens of true stories contained herein. Narratives about a quaint, little house that started as a corn crib for beer wagon horses. Inventions to keep your loved ones safe from grave robbers. The eccentric druggist who frequently sunbathed in the nude atop his South Side castle.

I am convinced there are many more unusual stories yet to be told. If you have an idea for one that would be appropriate for a *Columbus Uncovered – Volume II*, I would like to hear from you. If I use your idea, you will receive credit and a free copy of the book. Write me at JohnClark43206@gmail.com.

John M. Clark, August 2019

BEARS AT THE GROCERY

I N THIS AGE of internet shopping, an actual, brick-and-mortar store opening can seem rather mundane - especially if the retailer tries the same old gimmicks. Ribbon cuttings, door prizes, free gifts - they've all been done to death. But back in the 1930s, Big Bear grocery founder Wayne Brown found a unique way to pack the customers in – by bringing along an actual, live bear.

On February 15th, 1934 – during the Great Depression, nonetheless – the Coalton, Ohio, native opened his first grocery in a cavernous, 40-thousand-square-foot building that had previously housed a skating rink, a dance hall and horse shows. 364 Lane Avenue was a great location – across the street from The Ohio State University – perfect for walk-in traffic. Those who had cars were drawn to the modern, 1,000-space parking lot. Those who didn't drive took a free, Big Bear commuter bus from Neil Avenue or from the trolley line on North High Street. These shoppers were delivered to the grocery's front door about every half-hour.

On Grand Opening Day, tens of thousands, if not more, came out to see the Big Bear bear.

The first Big Bear grocery store opened on Lane Avenue, across from St. John's Arena, in 1934. The building had been used as a dance hall, roller skating rink and an arena for horse shows and polo matches.

And over the next eight years, no one entered the front door of Brown's revolutionary, new, self-service supermarket without catching a glimpse of it – inside a special cage, just outside the main entrance. Brown was so happy with the success of the attraction that the small cage became the bear's home for the next eight years. Caretaking duties fell to the store's janitor. An urban legend at the time claimed that any stock boy who made a mistake on the job had to lead the bear down to the Olentangy River and bathe it. By about 1942, the bear had outgrown his cage and was given a new home at the Columbus Zoo.

But other bears followed, if only for grand openings, helping the supermarket chain grow to almost 90 stores throughout the Midwest. And many of those stores hosted live bears for their grand openings. Crowds would gather in the parking lots to watch a bear walk a modified "high wire." Children lined up to ride the bear. On opening day of the German Village Big Bear store at 280 East Whittier Street, cameras flashed as a bear appeared to ring up grocery sales at a cash register.

At Graceland Shopping Center in Columbus, children line up on Big Bear's Grand Opening Day to ride a live bear.

Live bears garnered a lot of attention for the Big Bear chain. But there's no doubt that Brown, the founder, was also quite the supermarket innovator. That first store on Lane Avenue was the first grocery in the Midwest to feature self-service shopping. There was a restaurant, two bakeries, a flower shop, a shoe repair shop, a candy store, a drug store with a registered pharmacist on hand, even an appliance department. Customers would pay for items in their respective departments. Big Bear stores were among the very first to use grocery carts and motorized conveyor belts at checkout counters. In the 1950s, the company began conducting its bookkeeping

*A large, black bear at a check-out counter, during the grand opening
of a Big Bear grocery – possibly the one on East Whittier Street.*

on a room-sized IBM computer – the first in the nation to do so. And the company eventually claimed the largest refrigerated warehouse in the country.

Another stroke of marketing ingenuity was recorded in July 1955 when Brown opened the Golden Bear Shopping Center in Upper Arlington, anchored by a large, Big Bear grocery. The shopping center was named for the Upper Arlington High School athletic teams – which just happened to have produced golf legend Jack Nicklaus, who also became known as the "Golden Bear." Nicklaus' father, Charles, had been a golfing buddy of Big Bear's founder.

By focusing on volume purchases and relying on thin margins, the Big Bear chain consistently beat other stores' prices. Competitors saw this coming from the opening of the very first Big Bear store and threatened their suppliers that they would pull their business if the suppliers sold to the Columbus chain.   Big Bear found other, smaller distributors, but the strike lasted five years. The company didn't turn a profit until the fourth year.

A performing bear entertains the crowd at a Big Bear grand opening in Lancaster, Ohio, on May 18, 1960.

Ironically, the success of the Big Bear business model eventually played a role in its demise. Other, larger, grocery chains began springing up, putting enormous pressure on Big Bear to sell at even lower prices. Penn Traffic, a giant supermarket holding company, forced a buyout of the weakened company in 1989. Not long after this, Penn Traffic filed for Chapter 11 bankruptcy - twice. The writing was on the wall, and the stores closed for good in 2004, leaving many fond memories of a once-thriving, locally grown supermarket chain and the real, live bears that helped make it successful.

Before Cedar Point

I F YOU WANT to lose yourself in the excitement of a world-class amusement park, you can drive to Lake Erie for Cedar Point or to Cincinnati for Kings Island. But in the early years of the 20ᵗʰ century, you would have just taken a short streetcar ride to Clintonville. There, between High Street and the Olentangy River, was the largest amusement park in the country – with an enormous swimming pool and the nation's largest live performance theater.

The "Loop-the-Loop" ride at Olentangy Park was said to be the first in the country. But it was accident prone and was dismantled after just a few years.

An entrepreneur named Robert Turner set the stage for this amazing place in 1880 when he opened The Villa, which featured boating, swimming, picnic grounds and a tavern. In 1896, the Columbus Street and Railroad Company bought the property, hoping to increase ridership on its High Street trolley line. The newly christened Olentangy Park gained a few small amusements along with a reputation for being the most beautiful spot in Columbus. But it would be another three years, in 1899, when brothers Will and Joe Dusenbury of New Lexington, Ohio, bought the property, before the park experienced an explosion of growth and popularity.

"Racing" roller coasters were a big hit at Olentangy Park.

Recognizing the park as a weekend and summer destination, the brothers soon built a large performance theater, added a few other attractions and expanded boating facilities along the river. And that was just for starters. The next two decades saw the addition of two roller coasters, the country's first "Loop-the-Loop" ride, a "Tunnel of Love," the towering "Shoot-the-Chutes" water slide, a Ferris wheel, an amphitheater, small zoo, picnic grounds, playground equipment, rifle range, ballroom and a canoe club, where visitors would rent small boats and paddle along the Olentangy River. A spacious dance hall attracted the nation's most popular bands, like the Glenn Miller Orchestra and Tommy Dorsey. At night, the entire park was illuminated by the glow of 30,000 electric lights.

Olentangy Park's owners bought much of the "Fair Japan" exhibit at the St. Louis World's Fair in 1904, including the Banzai Bridge, and moved it to Columbus the following year.

When the 1904 St. Louis World's Fair closed, the Dusenbury brothers enlarged the park with the purchase of the exposition's Banzai Bridge, tea house and other buildings from its expansive Japanese exhibit. About 40 Japanese workers came to Columbus to re-erect the exhibits, and half of them stayed to operate them and entertain park guests. Staged sword fights proved to be popular, as was the Japanese restaurant. The gardens became known as a tranquil retreat where park visitors could escape the noise and rides.

The 1920s saw the construction of a swimming pool that could accommodate hundreds of swimmers at one time. It featured "filtered water," a diving board, waterfall and tiered seating for spectators. Sand was trucked in from Lake Erie to give the place a true, "beach-like" feel. As a convenience to visitors, the park rented swimsuits. When bathers stepped out of the water, they could dry off, put their street clothes back on and enjoy the rest of the park.

Olentangy Park remained popular into the mid-1930s, attracting 10,000 guests or more on a typical weekend or summer day. (Some have estimated the attendance at up to 40,000 a day.) But soon, economic conditions of the Great Depression began taking their toll on amusement parks across the country. In 1937, the Dusenbury brothers sold their holdings to businessman Leslie Leveque, who would later become co-owner of the tallest building in downtown Columbus. He cleared the site and replaced the park with Olentangy Village, a large apartment complex that exists to this day.

The swimming pool at Olentangy Park was said to be the largest in the United States.

Very little remains of the original amusement grounds. A portion of the old swimming pool is still used at Olentangy Village apartments. The merry-go-round, which was installed in 1914, was moved to the current site of Zoombezi Bay water and amusement park. In 1999, it was completely refurbished at a cost of one million dollars and later moved to a new, permanent home in a special building at the Columbus Zoo.

Olentangy Park wasn't the only amusement park in town. Minerva Amusement Park opened in 1895 as the city's first amusement grounds, near Route 161 and Cleveland Avenue. It boasted a roller coaster, water slide, dance hall, 3,500-seat theater and a bird museum. But the attractions weren't enough to compete against Olentangy, just three miles away, and it closed in 1902. The Minerva Park neighborhood takes its name from the short-lived amusement park.

Indianola Park opened in 1905 in the University District. It had the usual roller coasters and other thrill rides, along with a huge swimming pool and dance hall. The Columbus Panhandles professional football team played their home games there between 1909 and 1915. The Great Depression claimed Indianola Park in 1937, the same year Olentangy closed. The property was later converted into the Indianola Park Shopping Center. Today, the renovated, century-old dance pavilion houses a church.

Norwood Amusement Park in Bexley came along several years later and managed to last into the late 1950s. This was a small park with kiddie rides and a Ferris wheel at the intersection of Alum Creek Drive and East Main Street. Norwood was replaced by Main Alum Park and today is the site of a water pumping station for the City of Columbus.

Today, amusement park fans in Central Ohio will gladly drive an hour or two to ride their favorite roller coaster or to enjoy a musical performance or theme attraction. Few of them know that at one time the granddaddy of all amusement parks was located right off North High Street, here in Columbus.

BIG CANADIAN ROCK

A S A YOUNG man in the late 1800s, John Scatterday tried time and again to dig up the large rock buried in his parents' lawn near Sixteenth and Waldeck Avenues, in the University District. But he never managed to remove all the dirt from around it. In 1905, road crews began hitting the same rock while building Iuka Avenue. Rather than try to remove it, the men decided it would be easier to just re-route the new street slightly to the west. Out of sight; out of mind.

But not for long. When it came time to build sidewalks along the new street, workers were forced to deal with the situation again. Using construction equipment and brute force, the men unearthed what turned out to be a huge boulder weighing 15 to 20 tons.

The spectacle caught the attention of Dr. Edward

Dr. Edward Orton, Junior, who had a glacial "erratic" moved from a construction site to OSU's campus as a tribute to his late father.

Orton, Junior, Dean of the School of Engineering at The Ohio State University. He thought the boulder would make an excellent tribute to his father, Dr. Edward Orton, Senior - a noted geologist who had been among the first teachers hired at Ohio State and who, beginning in 1873, served as the university's first president.

Like his son, Orton Senior was, first and foremost, an expert in rocks. He was Ohio's state geologist from 1882 until his death in 1899. His contributions to the field of geology were many, and OSU honored him in 1893 by naming its new geology building, Orton Hall, after him.

Orton Hall, built in 1893, is the second-oldest building on Ohio State's campus. The geology building was named in honor of the university's first president, Dr. Edward Orton, Sr.

Orton Junior made a deal with the road crew to take the rock off their hands. He hired a man with a wagon and eight sturdy horses to move it about a half-mile southwest, to be placed at the northwest corner of Orton Hall on South Oval Drive. History is not clear whether Orton Junior or the Geology Department was to pay for the transfer. Regardless, once he had the rock on site, the mover demanded more money. He said he had not counted on it being so heavy and that the extreme weight had broken his wagon. Orton told the man that a deal was a deal, and that if he didn't like the terms they had agreed to, then he was welcome to return the boulder to the construction site. The rock stayed.

For the younger Orton, it was plain to see that the boulder was an "erratic" - an ancient rock from Canada that had been carried here by glaciers tens of thousands of years ago. Just how ancient became clear in 1971, when testing by the OSU geology department set the age of the rock at just over one billion years old. Erratics come in all shapes and sizes,

The Orton Erratic is estimated to be just over one-billion years old, having originated in northeast Canada.

and they're not particularly rare. But given the opportunity to display a fairly large erratic next to his father's namesake building, the younger Orton was quite pleased with his endeavor.

Orton Hall, itself, is something of a geological oddity. The university's second-oldest building was constructed in 1893, using 40 different types of Ohio stone. The rocks in the outside walls were laid as they appear in nature, with the oldest in layers at the bottom and the youngest at the top. Near the top are 24 decorative columns, each made with a different type of Ohio stone. And above the columns are 24 gargoyle-like representations of prehistoric animals. Orton Hall was added to the National Register of Historic Places in 1970.

As a side note, Ohio State has another connection to glaciers. Dr. Thomas C. Mendenhall, professor of physics and mechanics, was the first teacher hired at Ohio State, making him a contemporary of the senior Orton. Mendenhall became known across the country for his engineering achievements, and, in 1892, Alaska's Mendenhall Glacier was named in his honor.

THE BLIND MARCHING BAND

D ID YOU HEAR the one about the blind marching band that spelled out "Braille Ohio" at an OSU football game?

Actually, it's no joke. The Ohio State School for the Blind, here in Columbus, fields an honest-to-goodness, high school marching band. And in 2013, the young musicians, who might range in age from 13 to 23, realized their dream. They were invited by the Best Damn Band in the Land (TBDBITL) to perform alongside them at an OSU football halftime show, spelling "Ohio" in Braille while TBDBITL did the same in their signature script style.

The Ohio State School for the Blind marching band spells "OHIO" in braille during halftime of an Ohio State University home football game.

The OSSB Marching Panthers got their start in 2005, not long after incoming music teacher Carol Agler came across some old musical instruments in a closet. Credit the young instructor's naivete if you must, but it didn't take her long to realize the potential for a marching band – even if most of its members could neither read a regular music score nor see the yard markers on a football field. (A few band members have "low vision," and some can see "light" and "dark;" but most are totally blind.)

At the same time Agler began putting her unlikely plan into action, the Ohio State School for the Deaf, barely a mile away, was pursuing a similarly daunting goal of its own – that school's first-ever, high school football team. The school for the deaf invited the school for the blind to lend them their new marching band. And before you could say, "Right here in River City," the fledgling musicians had a reason to exist and the motivation to succeed.

First, of course, the blind students had to learn to play their instruments. As most cannot see to read regular music, they learn their parts either by ear and memory, or by use of specially printed braille music. Many of the students are helped by the fact that they have perfect pitch, something that is common among musically inclined blind people. Play or sing a note, and they can tell you exactly what that note is.

But the members also had to learn to march, and to follow intricate drill patterns on the playing field. This required some ingenuity on the part of Agler and the band's first co-director, Dan Kelley, who has been blind since birth. They enlisted the help of special, volunteer assistants – one for each band member. The assistant, often a friend or relative, learns the same routine as the student, and marches alongside them. By placing a hand on a band member's shoulder or in a special loop sewn into the back of each uniform, an assistant makes sure the routines go smoothly, and that there are no mid-field collisions.

Soon, the Marching Panthers were being invited to perform in a variety of parades and festivals. One Saturday afternoon in particular saw them rushing from a football halftime show to a parade, two hours away, and then to perform an outdoor concert. Quickly, they were in demand at schools, nursing homes, pep rallies and charity events.

A group photo of the 2013 – 2014 Ohio State School for the Blind marching band, believed to be the only blind marching band in the country.

Being the only known blind marching band in the world, the band quickly drew the attention of big city newspapers, television networks and local TV stations across the country. In 2010, that widespread publicity led to one of the band's biggest and most challenging event to date – marching in the Tournament of Roses Parade in Pasadena, California. Donations paid their way, and a physical therapist gave them and their special assistants advice on how to endure the parade's five-and-a-half-mile route.

With just 32 members, the Ohio State School for the Blind Marching Band was the smallest band to have marched in the famous parade in more than a century. And though they played loudly, the music at times was almost drowned out by the tens of thousands of cheering parade watchers. Afterward, one band member said now that he had marched in the Rose Parade, he could do anything. The pride was palpable.

The blind players have taken part in other nationally recognized parades since then, notably the 2015 National Memorial Day Parade in Washington, D.C. But so far, nothing has eclipsed the excitement of performing alongside the Ohio State Marching Band during halftime of an OSU home football game on September 21st, 2013.

As the Best Damn Band in the Land performed their iconic "Script Ohio" routine on one side of the field, the mighty Marching Panthers entertained the opposite side of the stadium with their very own, albeit much newer, tradition – "Braille Ohio," including the dotting of the Braille "i" with two blind sousaphone players. Band members couldn't see the 106-thousand standing, cheering fans. But they could certainly hear them, and many of the marchers were overcome with emotion. Afterward, band members were asked about their excitement. According to one young marcher, "It was freakin' awesome!"

BUILD IT & THEY WILL COME

A s a woman in her early 20s, Martha Wakefield became obsessed with architect Frank Lloyd Wright and the way he designed his houses to blend into their surroundings. She devoured his 1932 autobiography, later saying, "In reading the book, I had never found anybody in the world who felt about everything the way I felt about things." Martha and her husband, Richard, held onto every word when Wright delivered a talk at the Deshler-Warrick Hotel in Downtown Columbus in 1945. A year later, they paid a visit to the master architect at his winter home in Arizona.

The original Martha & Richard Wakefield house in Rush Creek Village, built in 1957. It measures only 1,000 square feet. Photography by Brent Turner / BLT Productions / Reynoldsburg, Ohio.

Inside the Frank Lloyd Wright-inspired Wakefield home in Rush Creek Village. Photography by Brent Turner / BLT Productions / Reynoldsburg, Ohio.

There, the three discussed Wright's work since the Great Depression on what he called "Usonian" concepts of homebuilding – smaller, affordable, "useful" homes for the common "U.S." family. As the couple prepared to leave, Wright gave them some curious advice. He told them to return home to Central Ohio, "buy a Jeep and build a house for yourself. Then build a house for your next-door neighbor."

Back in Columbus, the Wakefields nurtured a dream that began with Wright's suggestion. But instead of building just two homes, why not an entire community? In 1951, they bought 10 acres of land in Worthington – hilly and wooded and crisscrossed by streams – just the kind of property most homebuilders avoided. To Martha and Richard, it was perfect. Richard, who had designed factory-built Lustron homes after

World War II, would serve as contractor. But they still needed an architect.

As luck would have it, the Wakefields found in Columbus an architect who had worked for Wright years earlier, and who came to share their vision. Theodore van Fossen had gained local fame for his part in creating the Wright-inspired Gunning House, built on the edge of a ravine in nearby Reynoldsburg.

The Oscar and Edith Smilack house, built in 1960. It contains four bedrooms and measures 1,800 square feet. There's also a 500-square-foot basement.

Van Fossen would go on to plat the Wakefields' recently acquired land and design all but two of the 51 Usonian homes that today make up Rush Creek Village. For each one, he allowed the landscape to dictate the final designs – a technique Wright had described as "organic" architecture. And he borrowed from Wright's technique of creating odd angles, large windows and built-in furniture.

The spartan interior of the Smilack house.

The Conzoni house – one of more than four dozen Frank Lloyd Wright-inspired homes in the community of Rush Creek Village. Photography by Brent Turner / BLT Productions / Reynoldsburg, Ohio.

Each house design is unique, but many of the homes share common elements – flat roofs, concrete blocks inside and out, mitered windows and carports instead of garages.

As for Wright's other suggestion – to buy a Jeep – one former resident of Rush Creek Village can attest to that happening, as well. Brent Turner was a neighborhood boy when the Wakefields began their project. "It was a dark blue Willys (military style) Jeep," he recently wrote. "Dick's son and I would act as ballast as we sat atop a large sheet of plywood. This was chained to Dick's Jeep as he would drive across his property, dragging us along to smooth all the soil and dirt clogs during the landscaping phase of his first home."

Interestingly, for most of 2014, Rush Creek Village was home to the oldest living person in the United States. Emma Verona Johnston, who lived with her 81-year-old daughter, became the oldest American in May of that year. At the time of her death in December, Mrs. Johnston was 114 years and 117 days old. In her final years, she enjoyed exploring the neighborhood from her

Mrs. Emma Verona Johnston lived with her daughter in Rush Creek Village for the last several years of her life. At the time of her death in 2014, Mrs. Johnston was the oldest person in America – 114 years and 117 days.

wheelchair. Mrs. Johnston remained sharp and attentive up until the final few months of her life.

Today, Rush Creek Village is believed to be the largest community of "organic" homes in the country – a true architectural gem that has been placed on the National Register of Historic Places and which is virtually unknown outside Ohio.

A Coast-to-Coast First

THE ORIGINAL PORT Columbus air terminal and control tower sit empty at 4920 East Fifth Avenue – a silent reminder of a time and place that helped usher in the era of modern air travel for the entire country.

For the first 25 years of air travel, the skies were used primarily to deliver mail. Large-scale passenger service was not yet practical. For one thing, it was still considered too dangerous to fly at night. Those wanting or needing to travel from city to city continued to rely, mostly, on the railroads.

Then, in 1928, came a businessman from Canada named Clement Keys. Keys was an aviation buff who saw the future of passenger air transportation and set out to harness it. Realizing he needed some "star power" to make his dream a reality, Keys enlisted the services of famed aviator Charles Lindbergh, whose reputation was still at a high, one year after he had crossed the Atlantic in the Spirit of St. Louis.

Keys' plan was both simple and audacious. He would create a hybrid airline and train service that would transport passengers from coast to coast in just 48 hours, cutting in half the time needed to travel across the country by rail only. One of the first orders of business was to build airport terminals that could safely serve the newly developed Ford Tri-Motor passenger planes. That's where Lindbergh came in. He designed a network of 14 airports, with Columbus being the eastern terminus. In fact, Lindbergh chose the exact spot for Port Columbus and oversaw many aspects of its construction. Keys and Lindbergh called their new company the Transcontinental Air Transport Line, or TAT – sometimes referred to as the "Lindbergh Line."

On the afternoon of July 7, 1929, Lindbergh pushed a special telegraph button in Los Angeles. Three-thousand miles

The grand opening of the new Port Columbus Airport on July 8, 1929. It remained in service until being replaced in 1958.

away, at New York City's Pennsylvania Station, a light flashed, signaling the start of TAT's nationwide service. A special train carrying 17 passengers pulled away from the platform on an overnight ride to Columbus. The next morning, as the train pulled alongside the new Port Columbus terminal building, a crowd of three-thousand onlookers celebrated the grand opening of the city's new airport.

TAT's planes were named for the cities it served. Here, two of them, the City of Columbus and the City of Wichita, taxied to the center of the air field where they took on the passengers from the overnight train. The itinerary for the next day-and-a-half looked something like this: The two planes headed west, stopping in Indianapolis; St. Louis;

The City of Columbus – one of several Ford Trimotor planes purchased to help serve the new coast-to-coast air and rail service. Planes were named for the various cities that were served.

Kansas City; Wichita; and finally in Waynoka, Oklahoma. In Waynoka, travelers transferred to the Santa Fe Railway for an overnight trip to Clovis, New Mexico, where they boarded two additional planes and continued to either Albuquerque, New Mexico; Winslow, Arizona; or Los Angeles.

The new service succeeded in dramatically shortening coast-to-coast travel times. But a one-way ticket cost about $5,000 in 2019 dollars – well beyond the reach of most Americans. The uninsulated passenger plane cabins could feel like ovens while sitting on the ground and freezers as the aircraft rose to their cruising altitude of between 3,000 and 5,000 feet. Furthermore, passengers complained about loud noise and vibration from the plane's three engines. Pilots, more used to carrying mail than human beings, often steered their craft through steep climbs and banks, making some passengers physically ill. And frequent bad weather at the lower flying altitudes often forced paying customers to cover more segments of the trip by train than by plane. Many angry passengers began to refer to TAT as "Take a Train."

A brochure for Transcontinental Air Transport, Inc.

In the end, the service proved to be too ambitious. Planes were seldom more than half full. TAT lost close to three million dollars in just 18 months of operation. The stock market crash of October 1929 hastened its demise. And in 1930, the airline was forced to merge with Western Air Express to form Transcontinental and Western Air – the forerunner to TWA.

Though TAT was destined to fail, it literally paved the way for the future success of air travel – creating a nationwide network of air terminals and runways, a system of air transit radio communication and 50 weather stations, which helped ensure the future safety of air travel. Airlines that followed would also take cues from TAT's attractive décor, individual seats, reading lights, lavatory, a small galley and uniformed stewards who served meals.

The original Port Columbus airport that Clement Keys and Charles Lindbergh created served the flying public for the next 28 years, until a new terminal was dedicated nearby in 1958. The old building was used for a while as offices for private businesses and also sat empty for a number of years. Today, it is listed on the National Register of Historic Places. Concerned about its future, the Columbus Landmarks Foundation placed the original terminal on its list of the 13 most-endangered buildings in 2014. As of 2019, the future of the historic building is still in doubt.

THE EXPLODING PLASTIC
INEVITABLE

F OR MORE THAN a hundred years, the Valley Dale Ballroom
on Sunbury Road has hosted many of the biggest names
in entertainment. (See "*The* Place to Play" on page 149.)
But none has been as enigmatic or downright odd as Andy
Warhol and his Exploding Plastic Inevitable show in 1966,
featuring the avant-garde rock band Velvet Underground and
guest vocalist Nico, from Germany. It was the second Midwest
stop on the show's tour and one that would prove to be historic.

This mid-'60s promotional photo shows German singer Nico (far left) with Andy Warhol
(second from left) and members of the Velvet Underground. Lou Reed stands next to Warhol
with his arms folded.

That such a disparate group of entertainers would perform on the same stage was strange enough – Andy Warhol, the artist who painted soup cans and directed experimental films ... the Velvet Underground, led by singer Lou Reed, who was known to sometimes tune every string on his guitar to the same note ... and Nico, the model-turned-folk-rock singer who had appeared in films by Warhol and Federico Fellini. Warhol had persuaded the Velvet Underground to feature Nico as a "guest singer" on their first album. He dubbed the live show the Exploding Plastic Inevitable.

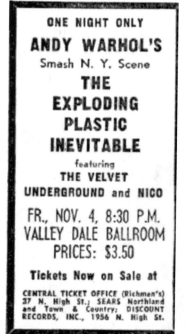

A newspaper ad for Andy Warhol's The Exploding Plastic Inevitable show at Valley Dale Ballroom.

A week before the event, a reporter for the Columbus Dispatch wrote, "Never in Columbus theater history has one attraction raised so much talk, created such a furor, speculation, interest and confusion. Some of the questions being asked are, 'Will there be actual explosions on stage?' 'Is this show an art exhibit of some kind?' And 'Is it safe to bring teens? Mine want to go.'"

If anyone in town appeared to "get it," it was OSU students. From the October 31, 1966 issue of the Ohio State Lantern student newspaper: "Lights, films, sounds, music, dancing, the Velvet

Underground, Nico, a pair of dancers, a candle, two whips, underground movies and Andy Warhol. They are all coming to the Valley Dale Ballroom this Friday." Tickets were sold at record stores and Sears Northland.

Very little has been written about the actual show. We know the ballroom was set up like a nightclub for the event, and dancing by audience members was encouraged. The Velvet Underground, who had been known to play so loudly as to damage their own equipment, were forced to wear sunglasses on stage to avoid being blinded by Warhol's stroboscopic lights. And throughout the performance, three of the pop artist's films were projected, simultaneously, on walls and behind the stage. At one point, between songs, band leader Reed, obviously comfortable in front of the overdriven amplifiers and speakers, offered the crowd this helpful advice, "If it's too loud, you can move back." Band member John Cale was later quoted as saying no one in the audience applauded during the entire two-hour performance.

Singer Nico on stage with Andy Warhol's bizarre, multimedia stage show.

And while we don't have a complete visual description of the performance, we do have something that has proved over the years to be much more important – a bootlegged audio recording of the entire concert. Just before the show was set to start, a group of art students entered Valley Dale with a reel-to-reel tape recorder. Instead of being upset by the prospect of an unauthorized recording, Velvet Underground's equipment manager actually helped them find an extension cord to power the recorder. The 105-minute recording ends with one of the students, Dick Felton, saying, "I'm afraid to play it back. I really am."

When he did play it back, he realized he and his friends had captured something unique – an entire, live performance of the Velvet Underground and Nico. And the quality of the recording, though not in stereo, was actually quite good. As Felton and his friend began to make copies for fans, it became the most-talked about, most-sought-after bootleg recording in America.

Even Andy Warhol, himself, wanted a copy. A few months after the Valley Dale performance, Felton and another friend, Bernd Baierschmidt, took the original audio tape to "The Factory," in New York – the name for Warhol's Manhattan studio. There, Warhol was only too happy to make a copy for himself.

Over the next several years, various versions of the Valley Dale bootleg would show up – sometimes on vinyl, sometimes on audio cassette. One was even titled, If It's Too Loud You Can Move Back. Then in October 2012, one year before Lou Reed died of liver disease, the now-defunct Velvet

Underground officially released the entire live performance in Columbus as part of a six-CD package. From tape recorder to bootlegs to store shelves, the official release was 46 years in the making.

In 2015, the Valley Dale Ballroom was acquired by a local catering company whose owners invested one million dollars into a complete renovation of the old dance hall. Used now primarily for weddings and large parties, it still hosts the occasional concert. Of course, it's nothing like the 1930s and '40s, when Frank Sinatra or big band leader Benny Goodman would draw well over a thousand paying customers. And even if it stands for another century, the old ballroom may never see another show quite like Andy Warhol's Exploding Plastic Inevitable, with the Velvet Underground and Nico.

FRAT HOUSE ESCAPES

O N A FALL afternoon in 1932, an elderly African-American man knocked on the front door of Ohio State University's Kappa Sigma fraternity house and gave a young pledge the surprise of his life.

The visitor asked Bob Thomas if he could visit the stately home's basement, to see the room where he was hidden as a runaway slave some 70 years earlier. As Thomas recalled later for a story in the Columbus Dispatch, "We showed him a rock-lined basement antechamber where he recalled sleeping on the floor. I wish we had asked him more about his memories."

The Kappa Sigma fraternity house at The Ohio State University. It is said to have tunnels beneath it that once led to the Olentangy River.

A tunnel, which has since been sealed off, reportedly runs from the basement of the fraternity house to below the nearby Pi Beta Phi sorority house, and then westward to the Olentangy River. The Olentangy was favored by many runaway slaves as a direct route north; the water masked their scent from any approaching bloodhounds.

The Kappa Sigma house is just one of more than two-dozen Central Ohio buildings that have been verified as "stations" on the Underground Railroad during the Civil War and the years leading up to it. Ohio had about 3,000 miles of secret routes – more than any other state. So, it's not surprising that Columbus and the surrounding area had many stations

The couple who built Kelton House on East Town Street were well-known abolitionists who hid slaves in their barn or in the servants' quarters.

and "conductors" who operated them. These men and women, some white, some free Blacks, faced fines and prison sentences for harboring and transporting slaves.

Early Columbus developer and landowner William Neil built the large, brick, hilltop home that would become the Kappa Sigma house in 1856, for his eldest son, Robert. Some believe the structure was placed atop an Indian mound, given the many Native American artifacts that were uncovered during its construction. William Neil owned a large amount of land in the area and later donated 300 acres for the establishment of what would become The Ohio State University.

Perhaps the best-known of the local Underground Railroad stations is Kelton House. When it was constructed in 1852, it was the last house on Town Street and surrounded by pastureland. Owners Fernando and Sophia Kelton were abolitionists who belonged to the local anti-slavery society. According to family tradition, runaways were hidden in a barn at the rear of the property or in the servants' quarters. There is a documented story about two little girls who were found hiding in shrubbery next to the home. Fearing that Ohio wasn't safe, one of the girls continued north to Wisconsin. The other, 10-year-old Martha, was too ill to accompany her and stayed with the Keltons for the next 10 years.

In 1874, Martha married Thomas Lawrence in the front parlor of the Keltons' home. Thomas had been born to free, black parents and was employed by the Keltons as a cabinetmaker. The young couple proceeded to name the older of their two children Arthur Kelton Lawrence, illustrating the close relationship between the two families. Arthur went to medical school and was a practicing physician in Columbus for the next 33 years. The Kelton House operates today as a museum with costumed docents and pre-recorded audio. The landmark home is maintained by the Junior League of Columbus.

The Hanby House in Westerville is well-known for being a station on the Underground Railroad. Today, it operates as a museum.

Another notable Columbus-area station was the home

of the Hanby family, built in 1846, in Westerville. Bishop William Hanby was one of the founders of nearby Otterbein University. His son Benjamin followed his father into the ministry, but was also a teacher, abolitionist, musician and composer. Benjamin gained fame for two songs in particular – the Christmas-themed "Up on a Housetop" and the anti-slavery tune, "Darling Nellie Gray." The latter is said to have been inspired by the heartbreaking recollections of a runaway slave named Joseph Selby.

"Darling Nellie Gray," which became an instant hit, featured the following verse:

Oh, my poor Nellie Gray they have taken you away

And I'll never see my darling any more.

I'm a sittin' by the river and I'm weeping all the day

For you've gone from the old Kentucky shore.

It has been said that the song was so popular that groups of soldiers on *both* sides of the Civil War sang it, though Confederate troops reportedly changed the lyrics a little.

While living with his family in Westerville, it was young Ben's job to guide runaways in the darkness of night from the Hanby barn to a wagon equipped with a false bottom. A neighboring tool maker named Thomas Alexander would then drive the hidden men, women and children to other safe houses in Delaware or Alum Creek, on their way north.

The National Park Service has designated the Hanby House in Westerville as a significant Underground Railroad site, and it's listed on the National Register of Historic Places. Today, the Westerville Historical Society operates it as a museum.

Composer Benjamin Hanby who, with his father, helped hide runaway slaves at their family home.

Columbus is so rich in abolitionist history that telling the story of every safe house or Underground Railroad station would require a book of their own. There's the home of Dr. James E. Coulter near North Third and Long Street. Coulter opened his home to runaways and held anti-slavery meetings there, as well. He once found a mixed-race boy hiding in his hayloft. The doctor raised him and had him educated.

The former Southwick-Good Funeral Home in Clintonville started as a church, where Reverend Jason Bull conducted Methodist Episcopal services. While he preached, his daughter would take food and water to escaped slaves hidden in an interior room.

Benjamin Bartholomew moved to a house on Olentangy River Road from New Haven, Connecticut. His home was said to contain a "floating flue." This allowed tell-tale smoke to be carried to the main chimney without revealing that there were runaways in the cellar.

Even Alexander Livingston, the man credited with

inventing the first edible tomato, took part in helping runaway slaves find their freedom. Many would hide at Livingston's home in Reynoldsburg, where he kept his "ark" – an oversized wagon used to transport fugitive slaves to Underground Railroad stations farther north.

Free African Americans were especially interested in helping the cause. Henry and Dolly Turk were the first Black family to live in Worthington. Henry had bought Dolly's freedom from a man in Virginia. Their home was used to hide an untold number of runaways.

The Caroline Brown house at Livingston and Linwood Avenues was another celebrated refuge. Caroline had been born into slavery on a plantation in Virginia. She and her two children were granted emancipation upon their owner's death, and the three moved to Columbus. Son Edward is believed to have built the house for his mother about 1854. He may also be the one who built tunnels below the home. Neighbors believed the tunnels led to a nearby barn and then ended near Main Street.

These are but a few of the verified safe havens in this area. We'll never know how many runaway slaves were aided by abolitionists in Columbus. But of the estimated 100,000 slaves who ran away from their masters during this period, about 40,000 are believed to have traveled through Ohio. With Columbus being centrally located and having plenty of nearby rivers and creeks for escape routes, the capital city was undoubtedly one of the most important cities on the Underground Railroad.

FROM CRIB TO CRIB

B LINK AS YOU drive past 41 West Columbus Street in the city's historic Brewery District, and you'll surely miss it – a blue, wood-frame house that wouldn't likely garner any attention except for its diminutive size. But aside from the fact that it measures only 350 square feet, this little home has a BIG back story – one that was written 70 years before the current "tiny house" movement.

The "corn crib" house on West Columbus Street, shortly after its conversion from an auto garage. Courtesy German Village Society.

A typical corn crib similar to the one that later became a garage, and then a cottage, on West Columbus Street.

In fact, it didn't even start out as a house, but rather a corn crib for horses at Hoster Brewing Company on South Front Street. The large, brick building that now houses Shadowbox Theatre and Rockmill Tavern originally contained stables for the brewery's workhorses. The small corn crib, believed to have been built about 1900, stood nearby. Cribs were common in the 19th century, when they were used to dry and store corn (on the cob) for horse feed.

By 1920, the days of horse-drawn delivery wagons were numbered. With the Hoster corn crib no longer needed, Franklin County Coroner William Heintz saw an opportunity. Dr. Heintz had recently bought a Marathon-brand touring car, made in Nashville, Tennessee. But his home in the 700 block of South High Street didn't have a garage. So, he bought a tiny piece of property around the corner on West Columbus Street, then bought the corn crib and had it moved to his new lot. There, he covered the slatted sides with barn siding and installed a garage door in one end. And that's the way the building stood for many years – as protection from the elements for a doctor's fancy convertible.

In 1948, German Village preservationist Frank Fetch and his father-in-law, Harry Royse, paid Heintz' son $450 for the property and building. Fetch and Royse closed the end with the garage door, then added a tiny kitchen and bathroom, along with a loft bedroom above the living room. The result was a perfectly livable, little cottage – cute enough to be included on the very first German Village Haus und Garten Tour, 12 years later. (As it turned out, West Columbus Street was never added to the German Village Historic District.)

Cozy? Or cramped? The living room of 41 West Columbus Street about 1960, shortly after its conversion from an auto garage.

Fetch was so taken by what the little corn crib had become that, instead of renting it out, as he had intended, he and his wife Elnora moved in and stayed for a number of years. It's ironic that, in a period when the City of Columbus was declaring many of the South Side's homes "unfit for habitation," Fetch was taking an old corn crib and making it not just suitable for a residence, but actually desirable.

Today, the little corn crib-turned-garage-turned cottage is owned by the Martin family of the nearby Martin Carpet Cleaners. And they continue to rent it out as a home, to this day.

As side notes, readers may be interested to know that the little "corn crib" house had another noted owner, as well as a celebrity resident. The man who inherited the garage from his father was a star athlete, and then a noted member of the faculty, at The Ohio State University's school of dentistry. While with the dentistry school, Dr. Bill Heintz helped develop the modern-day mouth guard for football players, which not only protects players' teeth, but also provides vital cushioning to help prevent head and brain injuries.

The celebrity resident, according to a newspaper columnist in the 1970s, was U.S. Marine Captain Richard S. McCutcheon. In September 1955, McCutcheon became the first top-prize winner on the $64,000 Question TV game show. He stunned television viewers across the country by correctly identifying the five dishes and two wines served in 1939 by King George VI to the president of France. McCutcheon's

Quiz show contestant Richard S. McCutcheon exits the sound booth on the old $64,000 Question TV game show in September 1955. A local newspaper columnist once identified McCutcheon as one of the early residents of the "corn crib" house.

win – engineered by unscrupulous television producers – invited scrutiny of the popular game show and others like it, helping to uncover an industry-wide TV game show scandal. The deceptive practices resulted in a congressional investigation and tough, new federal laws to govern game shows.

THE GREAT AIRSHIP RIOT

C OLUMBUS HAS A proud and storied past in aviation. The world's first cargo flight landed here in 1910. World War I flying ace Eddie Rickenbacker was born on Pearl Street, just south of Livingston Avenue. Curtis-Wright built 6,000 military aircraft here during World War II. And Bexley resident Jerrie Mock became the first woman to fly solo

June 28, 1891. Columbus residents rush the field at Recreation Park II, at East Whittier and Jaeger, when Campbell's gas-filled airship fails to leave the ground.

around the world in 1964 – beginning and ending her historic flight at Port Columbus. (See "Take That, Amelia!" on page 143.) And then there was the not-so-proud moment in the early 1890s when an airship exhibition sparked a riot on the edge of today's German Village.

June 28th, 1891 was a sultry Sunday in Columbus. Perhaps that contributed to the unpleasantries of the afternoon. After all, men were expected to wear two- or three-piece suits to special events, regardless of season. And if you were a woman, there was just no way around sporting an ankle-length dress and all the other layers of clothing that were hidden beneath. A few carried umbrellas to help ward off the sun. But they were of little use.

There was also the matter of the admission fee. Back in those days, 25 cents was nothing to sneeze at for a couple of hours of entertainment. Yet, they went. One newspaper estimated the crowd size at 500; another reported 2,000. Either way, it was a sizable number of spectators who filled the baseball stands at Recreation Park II, on the northeast corner of Jaeger and East Whittier. And there was a certain electricity in the air, as all who attended waited breathlessly to witness what was billed as the first ascension of a controlled, passenger-carrying balloon in Columbus.

The man behind the new-fangled contraption was Peter C. Campbell, a former jewelry store owner from Brooklyn, New York who preferred to be called "Professor Campbell." Fascinated by manned hot air balloons, which had been around for decades, Campbell was determined to design a far superior gas-filled balloon, which the aeronaut could steer with hand- and foot-controlled rudders and propellers.

The wealthy Professor Campbell spent years at his work, with varying degrees of success. In December 1888, he sent a newly built airship aloft on a test run over Brooklyn, with one James K. Allen at the controls. Using foot pedals connected

An 1889 illustration shows pilot Edward Hogan in an airship above Brooklyn. Winds soon carried Allen eastward, over the Atlantic, never to be seen again.

to propellers, Allen steered the America with ease from an altitude of about 500 feet. He landed successfully a half-hour later, saying he had never had a "pleasanter sail" in his life. The America, as it was called, came to be regarded as the first successful, pedal-driven airship.

Pleased with its performance, Campbell stored his three-thousand-dollar ship for the winter and made plans for a more ambitious flight in the spring. This time, he chose a 37-year-old Canadian man, veteran aeronaut Edward Hogan, to man the craft. Hogan had already made a name for himself with dozens of balloon ascensions – even parachuting from some of them.

In June 1889, both Campbell and Hogan were prepared to make aviation history with a full-fledged, high-altitude, controlled airship flight – again in the skies over Brooklyn. But after spending five hours trying to repair a leaky coal gas generator, the two had to admit defeat. Jeers from the estimated 1,000 spectators foretold a similar reaction he would later encounter in Columbus.

One month later, having decided to use natural gas from New York's municipal supplies instead of coal gas, inventor Campbell and pilot Hogan were ready to try again. This time, they had no problem filling the huge, 30' by 50' oval balloon. And the 10 a.m. ascension went smoothly, too, taking Hogan to an initial altitude of about one-thousand feet. But a short time into the flight, the eight-foot, horizontal propeller that had been affixed beneath the passenger car broke loose and fell to the ground, landing on the lawn of a home in Brooklyn. According to some reports, the giant balloon then overturned in mid-air, leaving Hogan dangling from a rope.

There are conflicting reports as to how long the airship remained over land. Regardless, it was clearly uncontrollable, and eventually followed the winds to the east, and over the ocean. Late in the afternoon, the crew of a small boat spotted the unusual looking aircraft, which had descended enough to be dragging the 800-pound passenger car across the ocean surface. As the boat raced toward the balloon, ropes holding the car broke loose, and the untethered airship shot upward and out of sight. It was never seen again, and neither was the pilot.

Little is known about Campbell's work between 1889 and 1891, but he didn't give up on his controllable balloons. It also isn't known what prompted the professor to bring another ship, and pilot, to Columbus in 1891. It's a fair guess to say he was on a multi-city tour aimed at rebuilding his reputation.

FIRST AIRSHIP EVER TO VISIT CITY

By 1891, Columbus residents had become used to the sight of passenger-carrying balloons, especially during state fairs. Peter Campbell promised residents a look at a truly steerable airship.

We also don't know how the airship, named Mercer, got to Columbus; more than likely, it was by train. The wide-open baseball field, home to some early professional teams (and Ohio State University's first home football game), seemed like the perfect launch site. There were to be two demonstration flights that day – the first at 2:30 p.m., the second at 4. 2:30 came and went, with the airship nowhere to be seen. But the crowd had paid "good money" to see the show, according to one report the next day, and most determined to sweat out the next hour-and-a-half under the broiling sun for what had been billed as the second show.

When 4 o'clock came and went with no sign of the giant ship, the crowd began to grow restless. Shouts of "Fake!" and "Swindle!" could be heard from the audience, along with a few calls for the return of their admission. But spectators were calmed somewhat when dozens of men were seen dragging a giant, uninflated balloon into the stadium from an adjoining lot. From then, the pace quickened. A trench was dug, from which Professor Campbell and the unidentified pilot tapped into a city gas main. Slowly, the balloon filled and stretched toward the sky, held in place by ropes tied to the passenger car, beneath. The pilot wasted no time climbing into the car and preparing for the flight.

According to one news article, the balloon and car rose to a height of 25 to 30 feet, and then just hovered until gas leaks brought it back down. Another article claimed the contraption never left the ground at all. Whichever the case, the crowd became enraged. And when someone who appeared to be in authority announced that the main they had tapped could not supply enough gas for a proper ascent, the audience had had enough.

Spectators howled and began demanding their money

back. When Professor Campbell and his associates refused, about 200 men and boys spilled out onto the diamond and did their very best to destroy the aircraft. They began breaking apart the car's woodwork and tearing giant holes in the balloon. Police who were called to the scene were helpless to do anything but break up a few isolated fights.

Not content with the destruction of the airship, some rioters climbed the large, right field scoreboard and began hurling tin signs that were used to inform baseball fans of the progress of a game. Metal was sent in all directions, barely missing some on the field. A few of the angrier witnesses shouted for a lynching. In the end, cooler heads prevailed and the crowd eventually dispersed, leaving the airship in tatters.

It is presumed that Professor Campbell and his pilot left Columbus as soon as possible. There are no reports of them ever returning.

GREAT GALLOPING HORSES!

FOR THEATRE-GOERS IT's difficult to imagine Phantom of the Opera without a chandelier falling from the ceiling or The Lion King minus the 18-foot giraffe puppets. But as elaborate as they are, such stage spectacles are not new. In fact, one of the most-complicated stage scenes ever produced delivered standing-room-only crowds to the Southern Theatre well over a hundred years ago.

A scene from Ben Hur as it appeared at New York's Broadway Theatre during its original production in 1899.

It was March 1903, and the most modern theater in Columbus – built of fireproof materials and boasting air conditioning, near-perfect acoustics and hundreds of lights powered by its own electrical plant – had been open for seven years. But for all the vaudeville acts, world-famous singers and touring theater companies that had entertained audiences here, nothing had prepared them for Ben Hur. The fictional religious story, set at the time of Christ, has been described as an "epic drama about an aristocratic Jew (Judah Ben Hur) living in Judaea who incurs the wrath of a childhood friend (Messala)," who has grown up to become a Roman nobleman.

The Southern Theatre on East Main Street is seen here about 1915, 19 years after it opened to the public. Interestingly, the car seen in this photograph was powered by electricity.

The book by Lew Wallace was published in 1880, and almost immediately there were calls for it to be adapted for the stage. Wallace resisted for almost 20 years, arguing that the book's thrilling chariot race could not be recreated realistically.

In 1899, producers Marc Klaw and A. L. Erlanger proved him wrong, and the first staging of the play ran at New York City's Broadway Theater for a full year. (Coincidentally, Wallace was no stranger to Columbus. As a Union general, he visited Camp Chase during the Civil War. There, he recruited men to go west with him to fight Indians.)

Producing complicated spectacles for a year-long run in a single theater was one thing. Taking the show on the road was quite another. The tour included 350 actors; 76 technical personnel; musicians and a trainload of costumes, props and

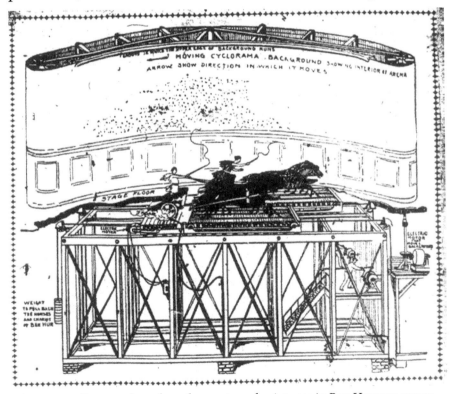

A cutaway diagram shows how the on-stage chariot race in Ben Hur was accomplished, using treadmills and a motorized cyclorama backdrop.

scenery. Every theater to host the play had to go "dark" for a full week before opening night, to give crews enough time to prepare the stage. Here in Columbus, carpenters actually increased the height and depth of the Southern Theatre's performance space. They cut large "traps" or holes in the stage floor; reinforced the floor to withstand the weight of 30 tons and installed an elaborate array of electric motors, flywheels and counterweights beneath.

Ben Hur's reputation had preceded its arrival in Columbus, and many residents had heard or read what to expect. The buzz had served only to heighten their excitement. On Monday night, March 16th, two-thousand excited theater fans filed into the Southern Theatre, taking their seats at orchestra level or in one of the theater's two balconies. To help accommodate the huge crowds expected for the show's two-week run, some paying customers were seated in temporary chairs placed in the aisles. The show was to start promptly at 8 p.m., and theater managers urged paying customers to be on time, warning that no one would be seated during the opening scene.

And no one wanted to miss the opening scene, in which the house lights were gradually dimmed to expose an ever-brightening Star of Bethlehem leading the wise men and their (real, live) camel. In the following scenes and acts, more than 300 actors could be on stage at one time. Orchestral music swelled and receded. Colorful, hand-painted scenery seemed to come alive beneath the modern, electric lighting. And then, the big moment – the opening of Act Five.

First, a low rumble was heard in the background, followed by the sound of horses' hooves. And then the curtain went up on the highly anticipated chariot race between Ben Hur and Mesalla. Each man rode in a full-sized chariot pulled by four horses. To accomplish the effect of a real race, most of the stage floor had been cut away to accommodate recessed treadmills placed side by side on separate railways. A 20-horsepower electric motor below the stage powered the machines. As the horses galloped in place, hidden ropes tugged at the treadmills, causing them to move forward or backward on the stationary rails and giving audiences the impression that the chariots were trading leads. A funnel beneath each chariot carried dust that dropped onto the stage as the "race" proceeded.

If this weren't spectacle enough, a second 20-horsepower electric motor powered a cyclorama at the back and sides of the stage. The huge, painted canvas unfurled from a cylinder at one side and was wound back onto a second cylinder, placed at the other side of the stage. The colorful backdrop depicted the interior of the Roman Coliseum with its thousands of race spectators. As the horses appeared to gallop in one direction, the canvas moved in the opposite, at a rate of 22 feet per second, completing the illusion of an actual chariot race.

At a prescribed moment, an invisible wire attached to a wheel on Messala's chariot was pulled and the wheel fell off, causing the Roman to crash just as Ben Hur crossed the finish line. The race lasted a full 60 seconds, with the horses' legs pumping and their nostrils flaring the whole time. They had just run the equivalent of one mile. The excited audience inside the theater cheered wildly for the amazing spectacle they had just witnessed. By comparison, the remainder of the six-act show played out fairly quietly.

A display ad from a 1903 Columbus newspaper touts the upcoming Ben Hur production as "The Most Important Dramatic Event in the History of Central Ohio."

So many people wanted to see the play that extra matinees were scheduled at the last minute. Special excursion trains brought theater-goers from surrounding towns. Society columns were filled with mentions of well-known couples arriving in Columbus to take in the production. And the show's popularity continued long after moving on from Ohio. In fact, the touring company of Ben Hur remained on the road for 21 years, with simultaneous productions in Europe and Australia.

Those early years of the Southern Theatre saw some of the greatest entertainers of the day stepping onto its stage – Lillian Russell, Ethel and Lionel Barrymore, John Philip Sousa, Sarah Bernhardt, Al Jolson, W. C. Fields and more. Actress Maude Adams portrayed Peter Pan in an early production of that show, flying from the stage to the balcony and back again. French-American dancer Isadora Duncan once said that if she couldn't perform at the Southern, then she would not perform in Columbus at all.

In the beginning, the Southern Theatre and adjoining Great Southern Hotel struggled to pay off its $1.5 million in construction costs. In 1901, two years before the arrival of Ben Hur, Fred and Ralph Lazarus bought the theater and hotel at auction for just $235,000. In the coming years, the brothers oversaw many renovations to the theater, including the addition of a projection booth and a pipe organ. By 1931, the Southern had transitioned to a full-time movie theater.

After several decades of deferred maintenance, ownership changed again, and for a while it appeared that the theater might become an apartment building and garage. Nothing came of that idea, but the theater finally closed to the public in 1979 – presumably to never open again. Then, three years later, Bill and Barbara Bonner bought the complex with the idea of renovating the hotel. They gave the theatre to the

Columbus Association for the Performing Arts (CAPA), which eventually mounted a multi-million-dollar renovation project, restoring the Southern to its original splendor.

The renovated theater re-opened to great fanfare on September 26, 1998. Since then, the Southern has regained its earlier reputation as one of the finest "live" theaters in the region, hosting intimate productions, well-known singers and bands. But a spectacle like Ben Hur, with its eight galloping horses and cast of 350, has not been seen there since 1903.

HISTORY-MAKING
PEANUT BUTTER

SUPPOSE YOU'RE GIVEN three chances to guess America's oldest peanut butter brand. You might feel pretty good about your answer, especially if you're familiar with Jif, Skippy and Peter Pan. But when it comes to the oldest, choosy peanut butter historians choose the one made by Krema Nut Company of Columbus, Ohio.

In fact, the company that makes it is so old, no one knows for sure why it's called "Krema." The name is thought to be an odd abbreviation of "American Refining Company." Regardless, it was started by a Dublin, Ohio, man named Benton K. Black. In 1898, he opened a small shop at the corner of North High Street and First Avenue, specializing in ground mustard and other spices.

Peanut butter was brand new at the time, and brands had yet to establish themselves. According to historians, the first mention of spreadable nuts was in 1890. That's when a St. Louis doctor began grinding peanuts into a paste, as a protein substitute for his elderly patients and others who had trouble chewing. Just five years later, John Harvey Kellogg, of breakfast cereal fame, patented a process of making the first real peanut butter, using steamed peanuts. Roasting, today's preferred manner of preparation, would come along later.

Benton Black of Dublin, Ohio, who started the Krema Company on North High Street in 1898.

Peanut butter was introduced to the general public at the St. Louis World's Fair in 1904, garnering an enthusiastic reception from fair-goers. We don't know if Benton Black was there to taste it for himself; but he certainly heard about it and began reproducing the manufacturing process within just a couple of years. The peanut butter frenzy is said to have calmed down a bit after the fair, but apparently the new spread sold well enough in Columbus to keep Black in business until its popularity soared again, during World War One. After that, peanut butter became commonplace in kitchen pantries across the country.

World headquarters of the Krema Nut Company at 1000 West Goodale Boulevard.

In 1922, Black moved his business to 1000 West Goodale Blvd. And through a succession of owners, the little factory has remained there ever since. In the early 1990s, ownership passed to the Guinta (jun'-tuh') family, including Mike and his son, Brian, who now serves as senior vice president. They quickly vowed to keep Krema peanut butter as simple as the day it was first produced, well over a century ago.

You'll find only one ingredient listed on the label –

peanuts. (Actually, the peanut is a legume, more similar to a bean or a pea than an actual nut, but who's to quibble.) Other companies add sugar or salt, along with hydrogenated oil, which keeps the nut butter from separating from its own, natural oils. Krema avoids that problem by using only premium Spanish peanuts from Texas, which produce less separation in the first place. Krema also uses an old-fashioned dry roaster, which gives the nuts an even, roasted flavor. Workers even remove each peanut's tiny "heart" - the bitter, little nub you'll see at one end of the nut when it's broken in half.

Not long after buying the company, the Giuntas set about to expand the Krema brand's offerings. Today, the tiny factory roasts 20 varieties of nuts (and legumes) and sells about 70 Krema-produced products like toffee, brittle and packaged nuts. A small café was added about 2001, offering a wide selection of peanut butter and jelly sandwiches, along with homemade peanut butter shakes. The company also does a brisk online business, as well.

The period between Thanksgiving and Christmas is when it really gets nutty in Krema's factory store, when thousands of customers pour in to buy nuts and nut candies to serve at the holidays or to give as gifts. Mike remembers a holiday period from the mid-1990s especially well. That's when so many people began packing the tiny store that there were fears for their safety. Mike eventually had to position himself at the front door, not letting a new customer in until another one came out. These days, the café is closed over the holidays, to allow more people in to shop.

Mike and Brian know they could make a small fortune by selling their property to developers along the increasingly crowded street in front of them and building a big factory somewhere else. But they don't seem too keen on expansion. And they don't mind saying they like it just fine where they are, thank you, continuing to make and sell the oldest peanut butter brand in history – one small batch at a time.

Now, about those "other" brands. Peter Pan was started in 1920 but didn't acquire the Peter Pan name until 1928. Skippy came along in 1933. And Jif, believe it or not, was unheard of before 1955.

Columbus resident Jan Clark (wife of the author) enjoys a peanut butter sandwich at the Krema Nut Company's café.

HOME DELIVERIES

J

UST EAST OF Columbus, on an old volleyball court at the south end of Whitehall Community Park, sits the house of the future. Or, at least, it *was* the "house of the future" when it was built shortly after the end of World War II in an abandoned airplane factory, nearby.

An original Lustron house serves as the offices of the Whitehall Historical Society at 400 North Hamilton Road.

With the end of the war came returning soldiers, the baby boom and a critical housing shortage across the country. Builders couldn't keep up with the demand for new houses. Several companies, including Sears, had already experimented with pre-fabricated homes, sold from a catalog. But demand lagged, and Sears sold its last pre-fab house about 1940.

Enter Carl Strandlund, an inventor and entrepreneur from Chicago. Strandlund had experience in building pre-fabricated gas stations. And he was vice president of a company that had been churning out porcelain steel panels since the 1920s. It was his idea to build an entire home with enamel-coated steel panels and steel support frames.

Strandlund formed the Lustron Corporation in 1947 and eventually wrangled 37 million dollars in loans from the federal government, along with a lease on the former Curtiss-Wright airplane factory at what is now John Glenn International Airport.

The new, one-million-square-foot Lustron factory was a

A complete Lustron house contained about 3,300 individual parts – all of which were trans-ported from factory to foundation on a single, tractor-trailer rig.

marvel of engineering, with almost a dozen enameling furnaces - each almost 200 feet long. The huge building contained eight miles of conveyor belts and huge presses that could stamp out up to 1,000 bathtubs a day. Each house kit contained about 3,300 individual parts, which were loaded onto a single, specially made trailer and driven to the construction site.

An assembly team from the local builder-dealer joined the pieces together atop a poured concrete foundation. Steel support beams were erected, and enameled steel panels

A promotional photo from the Lustron Corporation highlights the living room of one of the company's pre-fabricated homes.

measuring two feet by two feet were attached to each side. Panels intended for the home's interior were stamped with a wood grain pattern. Each ranch-style house featured multiple, built-in closets and cabinets, and a unique convection heating system above the metal ceiling tiles. Some homes even came equipped with a combination dishwasher - washing machine called the "Automagic." Most measured roughly 1,000 square feet.

Lustron buyers could choose from among four exterior colors: "Surf Blue," "Dove Gray," "Maize Yellow" and "Desert Tan." Most interiors were gray, though it was possible to choose different colors for different rooms. Buyers were drawn to the modern styling, the relatively low cost and the promise of low maintenance. With enameled steel inside and out, these homes never needed painting. Hanging pictures on the walls was a bit tricky, though, as it required the use of strong magnets.

Strandlund and his Lustron Corporation planned to build 15,000 pre-fab home kits in 1947, and 30,000 in 1948. But rising prices, production delays and distribution problems began to take their toll. Also, local zoning boards were wary of the impact of manufactured housing on established communities. In the end, fewer than 2,500 Lustron homes were built, and the company went bankrupt in June 1950 after defaulting on a government loan. In the end, 8,000 orders went unfilled.

An estimated 2,000 Lustron houses are still standing, spread across 36 states. Many, though, are being razed in favor of larger, more modern living spaces. The Lustron home in Whitehall Community Park was first assembled in 1949, in London, Ohio, about 30 miles west of Columbus. The owners donated it to the Whitehall Historical Society in 2000 to make room on their property for a new garage, next to their newly built, custom home.

HONORING THE ARNOLD

I T'S THE KIND of thing that would attract attention, no matter where it is. But plopped down in front of a convention center, along a major thoroughfare in a large Midwestern city ... well, it's a wonder the sight hasn't caused a few traffic accidents.

The sculpture, known as "Arnold's Classic," is a big hit with visitors to Schwarzenegger's annual sports festival in Columbus.

"It" is an eight-foot-tall, 600-pound, bronze statue of Arnold Schwarzenegger. Yes, that Arnold Schwarzenegger -

the bodybuilder-turned-actor-turned-politician-turned actor. He's depicted as he appeared during his "Mr. World" and "Mr. Olympia" days in the 1970s - striking a championship pose, with muscles bulging and his scantily clad derriere facing High Street.

A video capture shows Arnold Schwarzenegger at the 1970 Mr. World bodybuilding contest in Columbus.

To understand the reason for the statue, and for Columbus' love affair with the famous Austrian-American, we must turn the calendar back to 1970, and meet a Nationwide Insurance vice president who did sports promotions on the side. Jim Lorimer was working on bringing the World Weightlifting championships to Columbus. Ever the promoter, Lorimer had the idea of staging a bodybuilding competition at the same time. He invited several of the world's best bodybuilders, including the 20-year-old Schwarzenegger.

Schwarzenegger proceeded to win the "Mr. World" title at Franklin County's Veterans Memorial Auditorium that year, beating some of the top names in the sport, and taking home the grand prize of $500. The excited young man told Lorimer he was impressed by the promoter's professionalism and courtesy, as well as his organizing skills. He told Lorimer that when his competitive days were over, he would return to Ohio, and, with Lorimer's help, stage an annual bodybuilding competition right here in Columbus. Whether Schwarzenegger actually used a line that would become synonymous with him, "I'll be back," we may never know.

Lorimer was skeptical. But true to his word, Schwarzenegger returned to Columbus five years later, and

called on his old friend. With a handshake, the two formed a partnership that brought Mr. Olympia, Mr. World and Mr. Universe competitions to Vets Memorial for the next several years. Then, in 1989, Schwarzenegger told Lorimer he would like to attach his own name to an annual contest, and the Arnold Classic was born.

Today, the re-christened Arnold Sports Festival includes a num-ber of competitions, from bodybuilding to

Schwarzenegger admires the work of sculptor Ralph Crawford at his studio in Lewiston, Idaho. The for-mer bodybuilder commissioned Crawford to create three identical, eight-foot bronzes of himself.

power lifting, arm-wrestling to archery, table tennis and more. For one extended weekend each May, the event draws up to 200-thousand spectators and about 18-thousand competitors.

That's more athletes than you'll find at the summer and winter Olympics, combined. Cities around the world have tried to woo Schwarzenegger and his famous festival. But he tells them he has no interest in leaving Columbus, and often cites his 1970 Mr. World win here for setting him on the path to successful careers in bodybuilding, movies and politics.

Several years ago, Schwarzenegger was introduced to noted sculptor Ralph Crawford, known as the Rodin of the physique sculpting world. Schwarzenegger was impressed by Crawford's highly detailed works, and he hired the Idaho artist to create a special trophy for his Columbus sporting events. This was a bronzed, miniature version of the bodybuilding champ, which has been given to winning athletes every year since.

In 2011, soon after leaving office as the governor of California, Schwarzenegger reached out to Crawford once more. This time, he asked the sculptor to create three eight-foot-tall versions of the award. One was shipped to his hometown of Thal, Austria, where his boyhood home has been turned into a museum. Another was reserved for

One of Crawford's three identical bronzes stands outside a museum dedicated to Schwarzenegger in his hometown of Thal, Austria.

Schwarzenegger and was sent to California. A third statue was destined for Columbus, where it was installed in front of Vets Memorial Auditorium on West Broad Street. Schwarzenegger, himself, was on hand for the dedication ceremony in March 2012.

But the sports festival was already outgrowing the 60-year-old Vets Memorial, and many of the events were moving to the much larger and newer Greater Columbus Convention Center. Plans were made to replace the old building with a new National Veterans Memorial and Museum. In 2014, workers moved the statue to a small plaza in front of the convention center, prompting a re-dedication ceremony with Schwarzenegger, and the old building was demolished the following year.

Schwarzenegger's ties to Columbus have only strengthened over the years. He was an initial investor in the Planet Hollywood restaurant chain, which, for a time, displayed the tank he drove while in the Austrian military at its Easton location. The tank moved to Motts Military Museum in Groveport for a while, until Schwarzenegger decided to have it trucked home to California, where he continues to reward school students with rides in it. More recently, he persuaded Hollywood executives to film one of his movies, Aftermath, in Columbus. And he says more movies might follow.

But it's athletics that keeps Schwarzenegger returning to his adopted hometown year after year; and it's the statue of him in his bodybuilding prime that reminds us of his continuing commitment to our city.

A HOUSE DIVIDED

OR AS LONG as anyone can remember, it's been known as the "Brothers" House – a most unusual German Village dwelling with a rumored history that is just as odd.

Legend has it that the side-by-side brick homes – with a shared common wall – were begun prior to the Civil War by two brothers who had planned to raise their families next-door to each other. But shortly after they started construction, the

The so-called "Brothers'" House, now with separate owners, dates back to the 1860s.

two got into an argument – one so serious that it led each brother to complete his home on his own. Their choices of windows, lintels, roof, front door, even the very bricks, themselves, were different.

It's been said that shortly after construction was completed, both brothers were called by Uncle Sam to fight the Confederate rebels, leaving their wives to look after the homes. Unlike their husbands, the wives enjoyed each other's company and punched a hole in the wall dividing the two homes so they could more easily visit each other. Besides, they thought, if their husbands were to survive the war surely they will have made peace by then.

The two men *did* make it home, but they had *not* made amends with each other. The hole was patched up, and the brothers continued to give each other the silent treatment for the rest of their lives. That's the most popular story.

Another version of the tale identifies the two men as father and son. And that seems more likely. Hartman Debus, a bricklayer, apparently built the home – or, at least, one-half of it – in the 1850s or 1860s. His son Andrew, also a bricklayer, is listed as owner of the joint property some 20 years later. But there is no record of Hartman Debus having served in the Civil War. And Andrew wasn't born until 1867 – two years after the war ended.

The man who bought the side-by-side homes from the Debus family in 1941 once said he had the impression that the left side (316 East Beck) was completed first and that the right side (318 East Beck) was finished later. Regardless, the property was later split, and today, the two homes have separate owners.

Whatever the reason for the two sides being radically different, the "Brothers" House garners a lot of second looks from many first-time visitors to German Village.

IDA LOVES WILLIAM

O HIO LAYS CLAIM to eight U.S. presidents – men who either were born here or spent significant portions of their lives here. And there are just about as many memorials to honor them. But only one, the William McKinley statue in downtown Columbus, serves not only to commemorate the Ohio native's political deeds but also his enduring love for his wife.

Niles, Ohio-born William McKinley, the 39th governor of Ohio and 25th president of the United States.

Ida McKinley, Ohio's First Lady during much of the 1890s.

For most of his life, things seemed to go McKinley's way. He was a hero of the Civil War, having fought in – and survived – one of the bloodiest battles of them all, Antietam. He was elected Stark County Prosecutor, served seven terms in Congress and was elected president twice – while running his campaigns from his front porch. And he wed into a wealthy family, marrying the beautiful and refined Miss Ida Saxton, the "belle of Canton."

Those close to McKinley, however, weren't so lucky. Within a few short years of their marriage in 1871, the couple's two young daughters died; his vice president died while in office and Ida, who had long been considered "nervous" and "fragile," developed epilepsy and became completely dependent on her husband.

But McKinley's love for his wife seemed to know no bounds. Refusing to leave her side while campaigning for president in 1896 and again in 1901, McKinley had delegations visit him in Canton, rather than the other way around. While entertaining as First Lady, Ida would often be seen holding a bouquet of flowers – to hide her tremors and to discourage anyone from trying to shake her hand. She always sat next to her husband at group dinners, rather than at the opposite end, as was common. When he saw that his wife was about to have a seizure, he would hold a handkerchief over her face until her facial contortions stopped. Dinner would go on as if nothing had happened; and no one ever spoke aloud about the First Lady's condition.

McKinley was governor of Ohio when the state's top elected official was expected to find his own temporary accommodations in the state capital. The McKinleys chose to rent an apartment on the second floor of the Neil House hotel (the second of three Neil Houses), directly across South High

Street from the Statehouse, where the governor's office was located.

Neil House, Columbus, Ohio

While he was governor, William McKinley and his wife Ida lived in a second-floor suite at the Neil House, directly across High Street from the Ohio Statehouse.

Unable to go out in public without the governor by her side, Ida was forced to occupy herself for the many lonely hours while he was at work. Later, as the wife of President McKinley, she spent much of her time crocheting slippers – thousands of pairs of slippers that she would give to friends and acquaintances. Others went to charitable organizations, who would auction them for large sums of money.

As governor, McKinley initiated a ritual that would repeat itself every weekday morning after leaving the Neil House. He would cross High Street, and on the sidewalk in front of the Statehouse lawn, turn and wave a handkerchief toward Ida, who would be watching from their apartment.

Every morning was the same – a little custom that seemed to say, "I love you, no matter what."

The bad luck that had eluded McKinley finally caught up with him in 1901, a year after being elected to a second presidential term. While visiting the Pan-American Exposition in Buffalo, New York, an anarchist named Leon Czolgosz shot him twice in the abdomen. The president did not lose consciousness and asked that Ida be told of the attack in the gentlest manner possible. Surprisingly, Ida held up well as doctors and nurses attended to her husband. But a week later he took a turn for the worse and died the next morning.

The entire nation began a lengthy period of mourning for the popular president. And in Columbus, a group of influential people immediately began planning for a monument in his honor. Homer MacNeil of New York was chosen to create the statue. The Ohio State Legislature voted to appropriate half of the $50,000 fee. The remainder was contributed by the public, in the form of pennies, nickels, dimes and quarters. MacNeil drew inspiration from photographs and personal descriptions of McKinley, and from a man of McKinley's size and stature who modeled for him wearing the president's clothes.

On September 14, 1906, the fifth anniversary of McKinley's death, a crowd of 50,000 people crowded downtown Columbus for the unveiling. They were drawn by their love for McKinley and perhaps to catch a glimpse of the event's guest of honor, Alice Roosevelt Longworth. Alice, the daughter of then-President Theodore Roosevelt and wife of a congressman from Ohio, was known throughout the country for her fashion sense and her "tart tongue."

The placement of the McKinley Monument was significant – on the lawn of the Statehouse, where the former governor had performed his duties just a decade earlier. But there was more to it than that. The monument was erected at the exact spot where McKinley would turn every morning and wave to his wife in a second-floor window of the Neil House. In fact, to some, it's still known as the "Ida Loves William" statue.

Five years after President McKinley was assassinated, this statue to him was unveiled on the front lawn of the Ohio Statehouse.

Ida's health suffered a steep decline following her husband's death. She moved back home and was cared for by her sister. She did not attend the unveiling of the monument in Columbus and died just eight months later at the age of 59. Today, she is interred, along with her husband and two small daughters, in the elaborate McKinley Memorial Mausoleum in Canton.

The second Neil House hotel was replaced by a new one in the 1930s. The third and final one was demolished in 1981 and replaced by a new Huntington Bank tower. And the long-neglected Ohio Statehouse underwent a massive restoration, starting in 1989. But the McKinley Monument looks just as it did well over a hundred years ago, when memories of his unwavering love for his wife were fresh in the minds of Ohioans everywhere.

JEFF THE GIANT SLOTH

M EET JEFF THE giant ground sloth - one of the most unusual Columbus, Ohio, residents you're likely to meet. He stands seven feet tall; and when alive, probably weighed close to one-and-a-half tons. But that was more than 11-thousand years ago. Since 1896, Jeff has hung out just inside the entrance to the Orton Geological Museum at The Ohio State University.

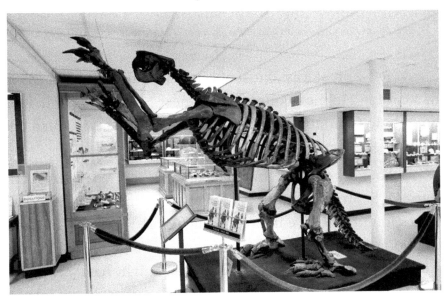

The skeletal remains of "Jeff," the giant ground sloth, are on display at the Orton Geological Museum at The Ohio State University.

This illustration gives one an idea of the giant sloth's height and mass, compared to that of an average adult man.

Jeff – or, at least, most of him – was discovered in 1890, in a cave in Holmes County, Ohio, near Millersburg. He was brought to Columbus, where scientists and artists recreated his missing pieces and put him on display.

So, how did he come to be named "Jeff?" We have our third U. S. president to thank for that. In the 1790s, unusual bones found in a cave in present-day West Virginia were sent to Thomas Jefferson, who was known to be fascinated by the study of fossils. Jefferson thought they might have belonged to a giant lion or tiger, and concluded that, whatever it was, it might still roam the western portion of the continent. When he sent Lewis and Clark on their famous expedition, the president instructed them to be on the lookout for these strange animals.

Jefferson's interest in the creature led him to speak about the unusual bones before a group of scholars in Philadelphia in 1797 - four years before he took office. Awed by the creature's vicious claw, Jefferson named it *Megalonyx*, or the "large claw." But it turned out to be nothing like a lion or tiger. Scientists soon discovered striking similarities between Jefferson's bones and those of an extinct ground sloth that had been identified earlier. This one proved to be a new species, though, and in honor of Jefferson, they gave it the official name, *Megalonyx Jeffersonii*. Our Jeff is also a Megalonyx jeffersonii; and that, of course, is how he got the name, Jeff.

Jeff, as you might suspect, is distantly related to the tree sloths found today in Central and South America, only much, much bigger. But like his distant cousins, Jeff was likely slow and awkward. In fact, he is believed to have walked on the sides of his back feet. And like today's tree sloths, Jeff ate only plants and leaves. The giant claw, which Jefferson assumed had been used to attack prey, was more than likely used to grasp food in tall tree limbs. And his long, blunt, peg-like teeth were useful for stripping leaves from limbs and shrubs.

Jeff and other Megalonyx Jeffersonii land sloths roamed Ohio and other parts of North America during the Ice Age, a period dating back from about 11 thousand to two-and-a-half million years ago. No one really knew, though, just how old Jeff was. The lack of any uncontaminated bones in the skeleton meant that radiocarbon dating would be impossible without

A Jefferson ground sloth as it may have appeared in pre-historic times.

drilling or cutting into them. But that little impediment was overcome by chance late one night in 2012, when a drunken 19-year-old university student broke into Orton Hall and broke off one of Jeff's claws. Campus police caught the intruder red-handed, his arms full of fossils.

As traumatic as this was, the incident gave researchers access to the uncontaminated bone they needed for dating the sloth. Turns out Jeff is about 11,200 years old – the youngest Megalonyx Jeffersonii ever discovered.

Incidentally, Jeff isn't the only giant sloth of his kind discovered in Ohio. Two other sets of skeletal remains have been found, including one whose bones show unmistakable signs of butchering by human beings using stone tools. So, although Jeff and his family weren't much to look at, they may have been quite tasty.

MYSTERY MANSION

I T HAS TO be one of the most tragic cases of unrequited love ever told. And if you've spent any time in the German Village area, you probably know at least parts of the story: In the mid-1800s, a young German man falls in love with a beautiful fraulein. A passionate courtship ensues and they begin planning for a better life together in America. Money is tight, so they decide he should go first, establish himself in the new country and then send for her to join him as his betrothed. All goes according to plan until the fairy tale castle he's building for her is almost finished, and she is due to arrive. But all he gets is a "Dear John" letter. His once true love has found someone else and will not be joining him.

Frederick William Schwartz built his mansion on South Third Street about 1880. Construction costs have been estimated at $40,000 ... or about one million dollars in 2019 currency.

The man is devastated. He stops work on the house and begins exhibiting odd behaviors. He withdraws into his own, private world. He refuses to cut his hair, walks barefoot just a about everywhere (even in snow), wears only woolen clothing against his skin, drinks only rainwater and, most shocking of all, begins sunbathing in the nude on the roof of his castle tower. In this tower, he dies a lonely and broken, old man, his body going undiscovered for weeks.

It's a powerful story, and one that has been written in countless newspaper and magazine articles. It has entered history books, and has been told hundreds, if not thousands, of times to curious visitors to the neighborhood. The tale is told about Frederick William Schwartz and his famed "Schwartz Castle," in German Village. And, as you might have guessed by now, most of the story is completely false. But that's not to say there was anything dull about Schwartz or his home. Quite the contrary. He was a fascinating man who built one of the most recognizable houses in all of Columbus.

Actually, William Schwartz (he preferred his middle name) was born to German immigrants in Niagara Falls, New York, in 1836. By the time he was 10 years old, William and his family had moved to Columbus, and were living in a small home on the very lot where he would later build his "castle." Louis Schwartz, William's father, was a German-born stonecutter who died when William was about 14 years old. As for William, he earned his pharmacy degree and opened a shop at Fifth and Friend (now Main) Streets, near Downtown Columbus. There, he mentored a young pharmacist named

George Karb, who worked in the shop for 15 years and later became Mayor of Columbus.

William's shop probably provided a good income. But was it enough to build a mansion and provide for his widowed mother and two sisters? Or did he inherit some of his money? Whereas other men's vocations are listed in mid-19th century census reports, entries for William simply state, "Own Income." Years ago, a man who had been William's neighbor told a newspaper reporter that Schwartz once claimed to have lived in California as a young man, working as a gold assayer for the federal government. No proof of this has ever been found, and it seems unlikely it ever happened. Nor is there any record that he ever married. He traveled abroad on at least two occasions - once to Mexico and South America and at least once to Germany, his ancestral homeland. Reporters have written that while he was in Germany, William saw a large, multi-story house with an attached tower, much like you would see on a castle. He apparently loved the home so much that he decided to build a near-replica back in Columbus.

The lot at 490-492 South Third Street was a deep one, stretching an entire block east, to Lazelle Street. It isn't known exactly where on this property the first home sat. But William left it standing, continuing to occupy it with his mother and sisters, until his castle was ready to move into. He also added a summer kitchen and an attached carriage house at the rear, both of which have since been subdivided from the original property and now stand as a separate, private home. Work on the "castle" began about 1880, when William would have been roughly 44 years old. The house today, with a completed fourth-floor addition, measures about 10,000 square feet. Various estimates have put construction costs at $40,000, or about $1,000,000 in 2019 dollars.

In stories written after his death in 1914, it was suggested that William fully expected his mother and sisters to live out their lives with him in the castle. He would provide for them, so that they could raise families of their own (under the same roof) and fulfill lives of leisure. But the sisters, it was said, showed no interest in social activities and were quite content to spend their days at home, cleaning and cooking. William was disheartened. Very little is known about the sisters' personal lives. One apparently had a daughter, as there is a reference to a niece's swing that once hung in the kitchen. Supposedly, as soon as she was old enough to be on her own, the niece moved out, and William gave up all hope of growing old, surrounded by a large, extended family.

Margret, William's mother, died in 1898, when her only son was about 62, and it may have been about this time that he began exhibiting what was said to be eccentric behavior. This is where myth meets fact. It apparently is true that he began walking barefoot - even in the snow; he wore only wool against his skin; drank only rainwater and perhaps milk; stopped cutting his hair; rarely spoke to neighbors or welcomed visitors; and yes, even sunbathed in the nude in the eight-sided solarium atop the tower, and perhaps on the tower's roof.

Many of William's eccentricities have since been

attributed to his strict adherence to something called the "Sanitary Movement." It was led by activists who had become alarmed by the filth and disease that was rampant in 19th century cities and who began trying to combat it. Without fully understanding the transmission of infectious diseases, they knew cleanliness was essential to healthy living.

William, in building his dream home, included many hard, smooth surfaces, which could be cleaned easily. Floors were covered with expensive tile, as were the walls of every room; staircases were made of iron. Also, by drinking rainwater, he did not come into contact with cholera or any of the other deadly diseases that spread through untreated municipal water supplies. William was also a strict vegetarian and grew much of his food on his property. He particularly liked barley, which he bought from the brewers on South Front Street.

Schwartz was buried in Green Lawn Cemetery, alongside his mother, Margret; and sisters Mary and Louisa. The whereabouts of his father are unknown.

In 1913, at age 77, William's sister Mary died. Sister Louisa, who was now 69, moved out of the house. And within about six months, William's own health began failing. His doctor made occasional calls. But aside from a few visits by his old friend, George Karb - by this time Mayor Karb - practically no one else was allowed inside. On May 11, 1914, as sister Louisa tended to him, the castle owner passed away in his fourth-floor sunroom. A group of Columbus druggists served as pall bearers, carrying his body to a waiting hearse. Louisa, the only known survivor, followed the entourage to Green Lawn Cemetery.

By the time of his death, William's once-magnificent castle was showing some obvious signs of neglect. Vines covered the shutters; gates were rusted and locked. The only access to the property was through a hole in a fence on his neighbor's property. And inside was a curious combination of discoveries: Expensive, rolled-up carpets - never used; bits of philosophical wisdom, in both English and German, written on the frescoed ceilings; eight food grinders in the kitchen; four barrels of vinegar in a sub-basement and stacks of magazines and other publications dating back about 30 years. The home was said to be sparsely furnished.

Apparently, William had not written a will, so the property was disposed of at a sheriff's sale. Louisa bought it for $3,800. It isn't

HOSPITAL OPENED

Columbus Maternity Hospital has been opened at 492 S. Third st. formerly the home of Dr. Schwartz. These physicians are members of its staff:

Drs. A. Livingston Stage, president; J. A. Rieble, vice president; H. C. A. Beach, secretary; J. P. Merchant, treasurer; W. P. Kyle, Ida M. Wilson, Harry E. Myers, C. C. Ross, P. W. Willey, J. E. Holmes, C. F. Frosh, Earl W. Euans, G. T. Meek, Ralph B. Taylor, Andrews Rogers, Robert B. Drury, E. R. Shilling, I. J. Mizer, A. D. Beasley, John Rauschkolb.

A few years after Schwartz died, the City of Columbus attempted to turn his house into a maternity hospital. Apparently, it was unsuccessful, and the building was soon up for sale again.

clear why, but the sale was later set aside. And within a year of the old man's death, the sheriff's department sold it again - this time for $3,755 - to a gentleman named Benjamin Manley. Two more years went by before the City of Columbus bought it, carried out extensive renovations and opened Columbus' first maternity hospital within its massive, 18-inch-thick walls. In fact, it may have been one of the very earliest maternity hospitals in the country.

But the hospital didn't last, and the city sold the building to another private individual. It was about this time that the old castle, like much of the neighborhood that surrounded it, began a long, slow decline. It eventually reopened as a seedy boarding house – home for up to 30 people at a time, one flush toilet per floor and no hot water. In the 1950s, two murders occurred here within six months of each other. In one, two brothers who had come to visit their mother got into an argument, and one brother stabbed the other. The other death resulted from an argument over money. One man shot the other in the head with a shotgun. Eventually, the city condemned the building, and the boarding house closed.

In 1960, a group of Columbus residents began campaigning to save the German-built homes and commercial buildings of the "Old South End," as the neighborhood around the castle was called. The city's first designated historic district - German Village - was established and so was a city-appointed commission, whose sole purpose was to act as guardians of all buildings in the 233-acre district. It appeared that Schwartz Castle might just be saved - especially when, in 1974, the entire neighborhood was added to the National Register of Historic Places.

There were attempts by other individuals to buy the castle; but prospects for making it truly habitable again proved to be too expensive. That is, until the early 1980s. That's when property manager Bob Echele and general contractor Bob Gease stepped forward with a lot of money, bought the castle, built an addition on the north side, added a fourth floor, carved out a five-thousand-square-foot penthouse for themselves and renovated the bottom two floors as space for an attorney's office. The roof for the new fourth floor, alone, cost Echele and Gease about 60-thousand dollars. They also narrowly averted disaster. In preparing for the additions, workers removed what turned out to be support timbers below the tower. This was noticed only when the structure began leaning. Emergency repairs were ordered, and a feared collapse never occurred.

The castle changed hands again in 2007, when realtor Mike Ferris bought the property and embarked on a second major renovation. Ferris, himself, spent hundreds of thousands of dollars on upgrades such as an elevator, ballroom and movie theater. He also added a whimsical touch - a "secret" room accessed by the removal of a particular book from a hallway bookcase. Ferris offered the penthouse suite for rent for $5,900 a month and set the sale price of the entire property at a little over one-and-a-half million. Due to a lack of interest, the rental price was later lowered to $3,900. Still, no one was knocking the door down to lease or buy.

This second major renovation coincided with the nation's "Great Recession." In the poor financial climate, no one stepped forward to buy the place, and Fifth Third Bank foreclosed on it in 2010. The following year, Scott Mackey and Brent Beatty paid the bank $715,000 for it. As of 2019, the two men occupy the upper two stories while carrying out maintenance on the entire building and making their own plans to re-renovate the first two floors. Under the stewardship of Mackey and Beatty, it appears that the old castle still has plenty of life left in it.

THE *OTHER* BLARNEY STONE

I T ISN'T PART of a castle. And no one suggests you'll acquire the "gift of gab" should you kiss it. But the Columbus Blarney Stone, like its namesake in Ireland, is the stuff of legends.

The story begins about 1960 in the backyard of a modest home on South Lazelle Street in German Village. Neighborhood boys used the mostly buried rock for home plate during their frequent, warm-weather baseball games. But property owner Jack Dempsey tired of ruining mower blades on it while cutting his grass.

One day in 1962, Jack called his brother Edward over to help him remove the stone from its resting place, once and for all. The two men dug and dug and finally unearthed a roundish, 350-pound rock. They hadn't counted on the thing being so big and heavy and didn't exactly know what to do with it. But one of the brothers – no one remembers for sure which one – suggested they put it in a wheelbarrow and push it over to the Old Mohawk Restaurant, just a few blocks away.

At this point, the story gets even fuzzier – perhaps because the Dempsey brothers used the occasion of being in one of their favorite watering holes to toss back a few brews.

The bar at the Old Mohawk restaurant, where the Columbus Blarney Stone acquired part of its legend.

But by most accounts, the small boulder made its way to the top of the Old Mohawk's bar. And there it sat for the next two or three days.

Finally tiring of the rock, restaurant owner Frank Broussard offered free drinks for the rest of the evening to anyone who could get it off his bar. One young man stepped forward and, to the surprise of many, actually lifted it by himself. However, before he could gently set it down, the unidentified strongman saw the small boulder slip from his hands and fall through the wood floor, to the basement below. This was at a time when the Old Mohawk kept live turtles in their basement for use in dishes of fried snapping turtle and bowls of fresh turtle soup. According to at least one witness, a couple of unlucky turtles gave their lives that evening – and not for restaurant diners.

What happened to the rock over the next three years, no

one remembers. But in 1965, the Columbus Shamrock Club took possession of it and christened it the Columbus "Blarney Stone." It's likely that the Dempsey brothers had something to do with this, as they both were fiercely proud of their Irish ancestry. Since then, the Blarney Stone has become a rotating "award" of sorts, given to the person the Irish heritage club declares "Irishman of the Year."

The 350-pound Columbus Blarney Stone has occasionally been on display at Dempsey's Restaurant & Bar on South High Street.

Some have kept the "award" in their homes; some have taken it to work with them. It has resided at the Franklin County Courthouse, the Shamrock Club and Dempsey's Restaurant and Bar on South High Street, whose owner, Mark Dempsey, is the grandson of original rock excavator Edward Dempsey. And occasionally, the Blarney Stone is "stolen" from its temporary home by other, mischievous Shamrock Club members. But it always finds its way back to its rightful guardian in time for it to be awarded to the next Columbus "Irishman of the Year."

So, while it may be somewhat less famous than that other Blarney Stone, in Ireland, the Columbus version never fails to entertain this city's Irish population. And you don't have to twist yourself into knots should you decide to kiss it.

DEFYING GRAVITY

D URING HIS ILLUSTRIOUS career, magician Harry Houdini frequently escaped from handcuffs, straitjackets and prison cells. And in his final, big act, he emerged from a tank of water – into which he had been lowered, head first and handcuffed – after 91 minutes. Sir Arthur Conan Doyle of Sherlock Holmes fame once said of Houdini, "Nobody has ever done and nobody in all human probability will ever do such reckless feats of daring (again)." Yet, for all the wonder and awe that he inspired, Houdini was not the best, nor the most famous, magician of his day. That honor belonged to one Howard Franklin Thurston, of Columbus, Ohio.

Howard Thurston (1869 – 1936), widely regarded as the best magician of his era ... if not of all time.

Thurston was born July 20th, 1869, in the family home at the corner of North 4th and Spring

Streets. His mother was the former Margaret May Cloud, a farmer's daughter. Father William Henry Thurston was born and raised in Columbus and fought for a short time in the Civil War. By the time son Howard was born, William was a wheelwright, making wagon wheels for the horse and carriage trade. But at times he had trouble supporting his wife and family – especially following the financial crisis of 1873.

Always a tinkerer, the elder Thurston turned to inventing, and came up with several truly innovative devices – a mechanical meat tenderizer, a curling iron, two-wheeled skates, a cigar-making machine and a fire escape. But he couldn't find backers for any of them, and his prototypes were banished to the attic. Young Howard and his brother Charles eventually made a few dollars by selling the discarded inventions to people on the street.

As an elementary student, the future showman and a cousin once skipped school to attend a magic show by legendary French illusionist Alexander Herrman. Thurston was immediately hooked. His cousin, Ada Thurston Wolfe, recalled years later

Howard Thurston began his career in magic by performing card tricks wherever he could find an audience.

that the boy was so excited he could barely keep still in his seat. It is said that from that day on, Howard's singular goal in life was to equal Herrman as a magician.

Howard started learning card tricks from a book, and frequently shared them with guests at a downtown Columbus hotel, the American House, where he had become a bellhop. He also joined other boys his age in selling newspapers aboard a passenger train between Columbus and Akron. Riding the rails was his eventual escape from home, where he loved his mother dearly but despised his father, who is believed to have beaten the youngster. As a young teenager, he continued honing his card tricks aboard the train, and then with traveling circuses.

The manager of a small New York theater eventually heard about Thurston and allowed him to perform on a real stage for the very first time. The manager was so impressed with Thurston's raw talent that he paid for the young man to travel to India and learn from their masters of illusion. He did and returned to repay his boss by entertaining audiences at his theater. This led to Howard becoming a big star on the vaudeville circuit. Then, as the live variety shows began to fall out of favor with audiences, Thurston moved beyond card magic to much bigger and more complicated, theatrical-style illusions. Each year, his shows became more elaborate than the last – so much so that by the end of his career, they required about 40 employees, along with eight train cars, to transport his huge props and stage machinery.

Famed magician Howard Thurston (left) and escape artist Harry Houdini (right).

Like Howard, the slightly younger Harry Houdini started in the magic business by performing card tricks. As Thurston turned to creating large theatrical shows filled with illusions, Houdini honed his new-found talent as an escape artist. The nature of his escapes – from under a river or inside a prison cell, for instance – meant he often performed in front of just a few spectators or witnesses; but the enormous press coverage he managed to garner for his stunts ensured that his fame would live on long after he died.

Thurston developed into a master showman, amazing crowds with illusions that he perfected and patented. He became known worldwide for appearing to saw a woman in half and putting her back together. But perhaps he was best-known for the grand levitation trick that he performed everywhere he went – causing a reclining woman to rise in mid-air and float from side to side. Thurston was fond of inviting audience members onto the stage while the woman remained suspended above them. Even from a distance of just a few feet, none ever detected the elaborate machinery that was required to make the illusion work.

The master magician once invited Houdini, himself, to attend one of his theater shows, and even invited him onto the stage, along with several other audience members. Houdini, alone, was given the opportunity to step even closer than the others and peek behind the scenes at the huge contraption built specifically for the levitation trick. Packing theaters every night made Howard Thurston a wealthy man, eventually earning him more than a million dollars.

A vintage advertising poster for one of Howard Thurston's magic shows. At their peak, Thurston's stage shows could contain as many as 18 major illusions, presented over a period of up to three hours.

But he made poor investments and financial decisions and died with little money. It probably didn't help matters that he married four times.

Thurston kept a grueling touring schedule, traveling around the world to entertain kings, queens and czars, as well as commoners. He performed for one week out of the year in Columbus, packing Ohio Theatre or one of the numerous other downtown venues with thousands of wide-eyed spectators. Despite his father having moved to Detroit and a brother having been shot to death here while on duty as a railroad detective, Howard returned to his hometown 29 years in a row.

Howard Thurston is credited with perfecting an illusion in which he appeared to saw a woman in half. This magic act, along with his levitation trick, helped make Thurston world famous.

On the evening of October 6th, 1935, Thurston played to a packed house at the Kearse Theater in Charleston, West Virginia, then suffered a debilitating stroke, backstage. Doctors told him his recovery would be slow. Thurston remained confident that he would return to the stage, telling those close to him that he wanted to produce a magic show on Broadway. But almost six months later, while still recovering, Thurston suffered a second stroke and then contracted pneumonia. He died in his Miami Beach apartment two weeks later, on April 13th, 1936. He was 66 years old. The magician's body was returned to Columbus, where it was interred in Green Lawn Abbey.

Thurston wasn't finished entertaining his fans, though. Perhaps inspired by rival Harry Houdini's similar promise on his deathbed 10 years earlier, the dying Howard Thurston told his wife that he would try to contact the material world on the anniversary of his death. For years, relatives, friends and curiosity seekers gathered at the abbey on April 13th to see if Thurston would keep his word. No sign from "beyond" has ever been reported. Unfortunately, the sometimes-rowdy gatherings may have eventually led to the acts of vandalism that severely damaged the historic building.

In a 2011 book about Thurston, noted author and illusion creator Jim Steinmeyer dubbed him "The Last Greatest Magician in the World." So, why does everyone remember Houdini and not Howard Thurston, of Columbus, Ohio? Steinmeyer once recalled the words of a writer who had known both: "All of Thurston's publicity was about getting you into the theater," he said. "All of Houdini's publicity was about creating a legend. And they both, of course, got exactly what they wanted."

One final note... Harry Houdini also entertained crowds in Columbus, but apparently only twice. His first appearance saw the escape artist emerge from a specially constructed packing crate, made and nailed shut by employees of the Lazarus Company. Not to be outdone, Hoster Brewing Company delivered a barrel of beer to Houdini's stage and had the magician locked up in it – along with the beer. Again, these were no match for the great Houdini. He escaped from both, with ease.

Rest in Peace ... Or Else

FOR AS LONG as people have been burying their loved ones, other – less scrupulous – individuals have been digging them back up. Going back thousands of years, most of the tombs in Egypt's Valley of the Kings were looted within 100 years of burial. This, despite the pharaohs having left behind explicit warnings and even curses for those who would desecrate their final resting places. More recently, and closer to home, grave robbers in 18th and 19th century America sought jewels and other valuable treasures that were often buried with the dead.

During that time, a gruesome, companion crime became common – body snatching. Body snatchers were less interested in buried jewelry and other valuables than they were in the bodies, themselves. The 19th century saw the number of U.S. medical schools increase from four to 160. And they all needed fresh, human bodies with which to teach anatomy and various surgical procedures. Supply and demand led to the unsavory practice of doctors paying shady characters in back alleys to provide freshly buried (or unburied) bodies. To the public it was, quite literally, a matter of grave concern.

The story is told of a woman named Sally Green, who

GRAVE ROBBERS CAUGHT.

Two Resurrectionists Arrested at Rochester With Three Dead Bodies Stolen at Oxford Thursday Night.

Newspaper headlines like this were common in America in the 19th century.

was brought to the Ohio Lunatic Asylum in Columbus, in 1838. She died in November of that year and was buried in the Old North Cemetery – the site of today's North Market parking lot. Some months later, when Sally's son came to collect his mother's body, he found only an empty grave, surrounded by other empty graves. When informed, local authorities had a pretty good idea who to blame – Dr. Thomas Morrow, of nearby Worthington.

Morrow was a teaching physician at the Worthington College of Medicine and had been hailed for training doctors here at the edge of the American frontier. It was generally known – and tolerated – that the doctor took bodies from the graves of poor people. But the Sally Green affair proved to be the final straw. Enraged citizens ran Dr. Morrow out of town and closed his school for good. It would be another 40 years before Ohio made it legal to donate bodies to medical schools or for schools to accept the bodies of poor people or prisoners.

Against this backdrop, two Columbus men stepped forward with novel techniques to prevent grave robbing and body snatching. The December 1st, 1878 issue of the journal,

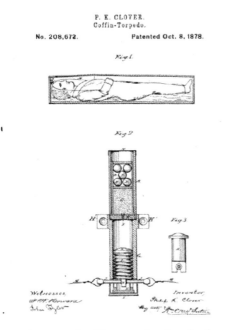

P. K. CLOVER.
Coffin-Torpedo.

No. 208,672. Patented Oct. 8, 1878.

Fig 1.

Fig 2

Fig 3

Witnesses
Inventor

The original, 1878 patent drawings for the "Coffin Torpedo," invented by Columbus resident P. K. Clover.

Scientific News, introduces us to an invention by a local man named P. K. Clover. Clover had recently secured a patent for a device he called the "coffin torpedo." According to the journal, the object of the coffin torpedo was to prevent "unauthorized resurrection." The article goes on to describe the invention in detail:

"The torpedo is placed at the head of the body, the lid is shut down, and the unconscious sleeper is, as we might say, prepared for war. A metallic hammer is coiled upon a stiff spring and locked by means of the bar underneath. To the extreme end of this bar wires are attached, to serve the purpose of tripping the hammer when the lid of the coffin is raised – and thus the hammer is released and explodes the cap at the upper end of the metallic tube upon which rests the loaded cartridge."

In other words, if someone should try to remove a body from a coffin equipped with Clover's torpedo, the device would fire a fatal blast of lead balls.

Two years later, a former probate judge in Circleville

patented what he considered an improvement on Clover's invention. Thomas Howell developed a method by which a shell would be buried just above the coffin, and wired to the coffin lid. This functioned as a kind of land mine, which would explode when the would-be thieves tripped the wires.

An advertisement for Howell's "grave torpedo" read, in part, "*Sleep well, sweet angel, let no fears of ghouls disturb thy rest, for above thy shrouded form lies a torpedo, ready to make minced meat of anyone who attempts to convey you to the pickling vat.*"

Experts believe these inventions were just a way to capitalize on people's fears for their dearly departed, doubting they ever made it beyond the patent illustration phase. But there *are* recorded incidents of would-be thieves encountering explosives buried near coffins. One such blast occurred in Mount Vernon, Ohio, in 1881, killing a man named "Dipper" and mangling another man's leg. But the placement of the explosives suggests that it was not a professional device.

Exploding coffins aside, there were serious efforts aimed at combatting grave robbery in the late 19th century, and one of them was also the product of a Columbus man.

In 1898, Hugh Clark opened the doors on his new grave vault manufacturing company and began designing what he called the first air-sealed, diving bell-type burial vault. It was, he claimed, "burglar proof." Clark's vault consisted of two parts – a flat, steel plate upon which the casket sat, and an air-tight steel dome that fit completely over the casket and latched securely to the plate. To reach the coffin inside, a person (or persons) would have to either cut through the welded steel dome or remove enough dirt to lift the entire vault and casket, weighing perhaps a thousand pounds or more, to the surface.

Dave Beck of Clark Grave Vault Company points to the advantages of a "diving bell"-type grave vault in this showroom cutaway.

The "burglar proof" promise was attractive to potential buyers, and the new, Clark vaults from Columbus, Ohio, sold well. Another benefit of the "diving bell" design was the vault's ability to repel groundwater, assuring buyers of completely dry interiors for their loved ones' final resting place. Clark's design became the standard for the burial vault industry; and today, most vaults are built on this principle.

Well over a century later, the Clark Grave Vault Company is still going strong, offering funeral directors across the country a variety of burglar-proof vaults in stainless steel, aluminum, burnished bronze and top-of-the-line solid copper.

It's interesting to note that the manufacture of metal grave vaults was halted during World War II when all available metal went into the war effort. But that didn't stop the Clark assembly lines. The company signed huge contracts with the U.S. government to make a half-million 155 mm shells, thousands of five-inch rockets, disposable fuel tanks for airplanes, 700 armored tank hulls and 50-million square feet of interlocking steel plates, which went into makeshift landing strips around the world. In helping to win the war, Clark employees simply tapped into the expertise that had gone into constructing their first burglar-proof grave vaults 45 years earlier.

SEARCH FOR THE SANTA MARIA

I T'S HARD TO imagine a more ignominious final chapter in the story of a once-celebrated "star" of the city's downtown riverfront. The Santa Maria – a full-size replica of the sailing ship Christopher Columbus once captained – in pieces and out of public view, rotting away beside a wastewater treatment plant. How did she fall so far?

In the late 1980s, the City of Columbus began making big plans to mark the 500th anniversary of the famous voyage

The replica Santa Maria was believed to be the most accurate re-construction of Christopher Columbus' flagship sailing vessel.

made by its namesake explorer. One of the highlights of the 1992 celebration would be the United States' first-ever international flower show, AmeriFlora. Another was the commission of a permanent riverfront attraction – a replica of the famous Santa Maria, which Columbus had sailed to the "New World."

One-and-a-half million dollars was raised through private donations, and a boat building company in Albany, New York, was hired to build the 97-foot-long, three-masted ship. Once completed in 1991, the builders separated it into two halves and transported it by truck to the parking lot of the old Veterans Memorial Coliseum on West Broad Street. There, it was reassembled and moved to the east side of the Scioto River, where it was moored at Battelle Park.

The Santa Maria replica was an instant hit with local citizens. President George H. W. Bush referenced it in remarks at the opening of AmeriFlora in April of the following year. Columbus leaders called it "an inspiration to us all" and a "lifetime legacy" for the City of Columbus. The ship became a floating museum, welcoming visitors from all over the world and hosting countless overnight campouts by scouts and other youth groups.

Over the years, the number of annual visitors fell from the hundreds of thousands to about 17,000. Admission fees were not enough to pay for the ship's upkeep. In 2011, the non-profit group that owned the ship went out of business, and ownership of the Santa Maria passed to the City of

Columbus. When the city made plans to revamp the riverfront a few years later, the ship had to be pulled from the water.

At first, city leaders planned for it to be a temporary removal. They knew repairs would be needed, given that some of the wooden planking had decayed over the years. But they pointed to the fiberglass construction of the boat's bottom as reason why the repairs would be limited ... and not too costly. There was talk of eventually moving the replica to the other side of the river, near COSI. Then, reality set in.

Repair estimates swelled to one million dollars – about two-thirds of the original construction cost. The city, which had just spent $500,000 to move the Santa Maria into drydock, was not interested in footing such a large repair bill.

In 2014, the boat that once was declared "the world's most authentic, museum-quality representation of the Santa Maria" was taken apart and moved 11 miles south, to a field next to the Southerly Wastewater Treatment Plant in Lockbourne. There it rests in 10 pieces, partially covered in tarps – not exactly the future that had been envisioned just a quarter of a century earlier.

Built at a cost of one-and-a-half million dollars, the Santa Maria needs about a million dollars in repairs. So far, no one has stepped forward with that kind of donation.

This satellite photo shows the Santa Maria replica in pieces next to a wastewater treatment plant in Lockbourne.

THE 'SHOE IN CHURCH

FRANKLIN ART GLASS has received some odd requests over the years. There was the stained-glass bathroom it created for Hustler Magazine founder Larry Flynt and the 45,000 Tiffany-style lampshades for Wendy's restaurants. But perhaps the most unusual order was the one that came from a historic downtown Columbus church in the mid-1960s.

"Old Trinity," as the downtown Trinity Episcopal Church is sometimes known, was built in 1866.

The rector of Trinity Episcopal Church at Broad and Third wanted a new set of windows for the front of the 100-year-old building – one that included depictions of Ohio Stadium (often referred to as the "Horseshoe"), the LaVeque Tower and more than a dozen other local landmarks.

Some parishioners found it a little disconcerting to look up and see the Christopher Columbus statue at City Hall instead of Jesus speaking to his followers. But Roger Nichols, Trinity rector from 1960 to 1969, thought it was completely logical. As he saw it, congregants would look at the windows as they left church services and be reminded to carry the sermon's message out into secular society. Nichols named the window, "The Church in the World."

The large rose medallions at the top of the windows feature city, state and U.S. flags, dramatizing the calling of Christians as citizens of Columbus, the State of Ohio and the United States. Each of the tall, narrow windows below the medallions, called "lancet" windows, has a separate theme. Look closely and you'll see the Ohio Statehouse, a buckeye, an Ohio farm, an I-71 sign, downtown skyscrapers, the main library, City Hall, Port Columbus Airport, the OSU Medical Center, even the previous COSI building on East Broad Street and the old Veterans Memorial building on West Broad.

The "Church in the World" window at Trinity Episcopal Church was crafted by Franklin Art Glass and installed in 1965.

In 1970, Trinity Episcopal installed a new organ with more than 3,600 pipes at the front of the church. Its installation meant obscuring many of the modern depictions from worshiping parishioners. And while that suited some church members just fine, the rector then had the windows lit from the inside so that passersby could enjoy them from the outside at night.

Despite the modern

depictions, Trinity Episcopal has a long history in Columbus. In fact, many refer to it as "Old Trinity," to distinguish it from Trinity Lutheran Church on South Third Street. Its first congregation met in May 1817, just one year after Columbus was officially declared a city. The building you see today was constructed in 1866.

Besides its totally modern stained glass windows, Old Trinity has one other claim to fame. In 1871 it was the site of this city's only royal wedding. May Parsons, the daughter of early Columbus millionaire George Parsons, married Prince Ernst Manderup Alexander zu Lynar of Prussia. The two had met in Paris while Miss Parsons was on a tour of Europe with her mother.

Local landmarks, as seen in panels from the "Church in the World" stained glass window at Trinity Episcopal Church, downtown Columbus.

The Ohio Statehouse, as seen in stained glass at Old Trinity Church.

State Flag Landmark

STRAIGHT TO THE POORHOUSE

MANY OF US baby boomers grew up hearing our parents exclaim, "You're driving us to the poorhouse!" If we had lived on Columbus' near south side in the mid-nineteenth century, Mom and Dad would not have had far to go. Simply turn south from Livingston Avenue onto Lathrop Street, and you would have run right into the Franklin County Poor House, where the now-vacant Beck Elementary School stands today. In fact, maps from the mid-nineteenth century denote today's Lathrop Street as "Poor House Lane."

Renamed the "Franklin County Infirmary" in 1850, the county's second poorhouse was a taxpayer-supported institution that housed up to 260 poor and disabled residents, mostly older ones. Poorhouses were common throughout the United States prior to 1935 and the passage of the Social Security Act, which shifted much of the responsibility for the indigent from counties to the federal government. The main poorhouse building and several associated structures sat on an eleven-acre tract from Beck Street on the north to Sycamore Street on the south between Briggs and South Ninth Streets. Built about 1839, it was just outside the present-day German Village Historic District.

In 1867, the Ohio legislature called for the creation of a State Board of Charities to monitor conditions at publicly supported jails and infirmaries. The first report on the county infirmary came a year later. It showed the residents to consist of "80 infirm and indigent persons, 53 insane and idiotic people and 30 orphans under care." The so-called insane were housed on the upper floor of a smaller separate two-story building. While conditions for the general population were only hinted at, they must have been far better than those for the insane, "for whom any conceivable change of horrors would be a relief," the report stated.

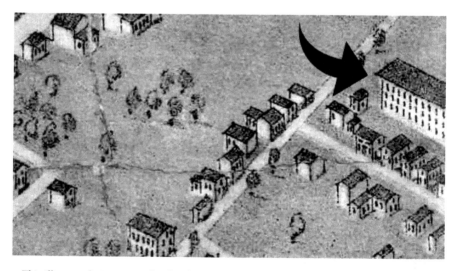

This illustrated 1872 map of Columbus shows the location and general outline of the Poor House's main building – where the old Beck Street School building sits today.

On the afternoon of June 27, 1878, fire broke out in the kitchen of the main building, quickly spread to the roof and forced the county to find temporary lodging for most of the 260 "inmates." Many went to nearby homes. Though repairs were made, it was clear that a new facility was needed. In 1882, the Franklin County Commission authorized the purchase of 98 acres of land along what is now Alum Creek Drive. And on November 6, 1883, residents were moved to the larger and more modern county infirmary, a facility that would be used for the next 85 years.

For a while, there were efforts to use the main poorhouse building as a school. However, workers had significantly weakened the structure while carving out classroom space, and it soon became apparent that it had to go. Within about a year, Beck Street School was being built to replace the main structure, with the rest of the property being divided into residential lots.

For years, there were rumors that a house near Beck School sat on part of the foundation of the original Poor House's main building ... and that there were "cells" in the basement. In December 2017, the author of this book was directed to a 19th century "double" at 684-686 Lathrop Street, directly south of the Beck School parking lot. The owner of the rental property, who said he hadn't visited the building's basement in more than 20 years, agreed to meet me at the property.

We opened a pair of external, metal doors leading to the basement of 684 – the unit closer to the school. Along the north wall were four tiny rooms, apparently fashioned from the same limestone rubble that made up the building's foundation. Each room was no larger than 8 feet by 10 feet. One had a heavy, wood door. It was easy to imagine these tiny rooms as the "cells" that had been rumored about over the

Beck Street School was built in 1884 on the site of the old Poor House.

years. The case for this being a part of the old Poorhouse was strengthened a year later, when I discovered a newspaper article from the mid-1930s identifying this very structure as being the "last remaining" building of the old complex.

Though the horrors of the old institution have long faded from memory, other little reminders still pop up from time to time. While excavating school grounds in April 1966, workers discovered huge shackle chains, the kind once used to restrain people. And as one might suspect, both the old Beck Street School and at least two neighboring houses are said to be haunted.

A 1935 newspaper article identifies this "double" residence at 684-686 Briggs Street as being an original Poorhouse building.

One of the four tiny rooms (or cells?) in the basement of 684 Briggs Street – the northern half of the building identified as having been part of the old Poor House.

TAKE *THAT*, AMELIA!

GIVEN THE LOVE for all things sports in Columbus, you would be excused for first thinking the statue at John Glenn International Airport represents a women's basketball coach. But that's no ball the woman is holding. It's planet Earth, as in the one she circled in a single-engine plane, by herself, in 1964.

From the time Jerrie Mock took a short plane ride with her father at the age of five, the Newark, Ohio, native knew flying was in her blood. As a college student, she studied aeronautical engineering at The Ohio State University – the only woman in her class – and the only chemistry student to receive perfect test scores.

At age 20, Mock, for reasons that aren't entirely clear, gave up her dreams and dropped out of college. She married an advertising executive, took up residence in Bexley and began raising three children. But thoughts of flying were never far from her mind, and in 1958 she earned her private pilot license. Husband Russ Mock also received his, and soon the couple were half-owners of a decade old, single-engine Cessna with unreliable brakes and a fresh paint job to cover the cracks.

When Mock told her husband she was bored sitting at

home all day, he said, "Maybe you should get in your plane and just fly around the world." Russ was joking. But Jerrie took it seriously and began to contemplate the possibility. Soon, she was onboard with the idea. Making her plans in 1963, she didn't even realize at first that no woman had ever done what she was about to attempt – to complete a solo plane trip around the globe. Amelia Earhart had tried to fly around the world 26 years earlier – but in a much-more sophisticated airplane and with a navigator on board. It was on that attempt that Earhart disappeared.

Mock's year-long preparations involved planning 19 separate touchdowns in about as many countries. Flight plans had to be filed. Maps were drawn. Foreign embassies had to be informed, lest they mistake her for a spy and have her shot down. Then there was the issue of expenses. Russ, ever the promoter, persuaded the Columbus Dispatch to help finance the trip in exchange for exclusive stories from along the route.

Jerrie Mock, dubbed the "Flying Housewife," poses with the single-engine Cessna she flew around the world in 1964.

Mock dubbed her plane the Spirit of Columbus. And on March 19th, 1964, after dropping her children off with her mother-in-law, she climbed into the cramped cockpit and took off. "Cramped" because the three other seats in the small plane had been removed and replaced with fuel tanks so that she could make it over the oceans.

Heading east, Mock encountered problems almost immediately. Thick clouds prevented her from making visual assessments of her location. Two onboard directional finders registered 60 degrees apart. Her high-frequency radio would not operate. She overshot her first destination, Bermuda, and had to turn around. Upon landing, winds were so strong that she had to put the weight of her entire 100-pound body on the brakes. And crewmen on the ground had to help stabilize the plane as it literally spun around in the wind. While in Bermuda she had the radio checked out. Someone had deliberately disconnected it.

After such an exhausting and dangerous first leg, few would have blamed Jerrie for giving up. But she persevered. Days were long; stops were short. She washed her one blouse and skirt in hotel room sinks. Weather delays and equipment malfunctions persisted. Then, four weeks later, she made her final refueling stop, in Bowling Green, Kentucky. Russ radioed his wife to ask when she would be home, as the governor, the Federal Aviation Administrator and several thousand fans were waiting to welcome her.

Mock landed at Port Columbus Airport on April 17th,

1964, 29 days and 23-thousand miles after she had started. She had set seven aviation records, including the first woman to fly over both the Atlantic and Pacific Oceans. A month later, Mock and her family traveled to Washington, D.C., where President Johnson awarded her the FAA's prestigious Exceptional Service Decoration.

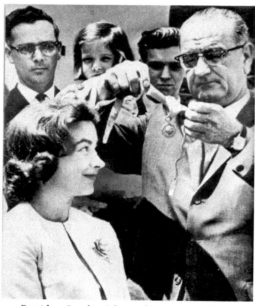

President Lyndon Johnson bestows upon Jerrie Mock a prestigious medal from the Federal Aviation Administration.

Many expected Mock's fame to continue. One TV game show host went so far as to suggest Doris Day would portray her in a movie about her incredible feat. But no movie offers came. Mock continued to fly, and she set more records. But the public soon forgot about her. Some have speculated that the turbulence of the '60s diverted attention away from her. Mock eventually divorced her husband, moved to Florida and bought a small house with her divorce settlement. Even her neighbors didn't know she was a record-setting aviatrix.

On April 17th, 2014, exactly 50 years from the day she

finished her famous flight, Jerrie Mock was honored with a sculpture by local artist Renate Fackler at Port Columbus Airport. (Columbus would honor another local aviator, John Glenn, by re-naming the airport in his honor two years later.) Mock didn't attend the unveiling ceremony, but she did send greetings by video: "Columbus is a great community, and I appreciate all that you are doing to respect its history and to bring an even better future. Long live the spirit of Columbus."

A full-sized statue of record-setting aviatrix Jerrie Mock welcomes visitors at the John Glenn International Airport in Columbus, Ohio.

Jerrie Mock died five months later, at the age of 88. At her request, her ashes were scattered over the Gulf of Mexico. And the Spirit of Columbus? In 1975, it was donated to the

National Air and Space Museum. Today, you can see it at the museum's Steven F. Udvar-Hazy Center in Chantilly, Virginia.

THE PLACE TO PLAY

I N A CITY seemingly saturated with "event spaces," one stands out for being more than two centuries in the making.

The year was 1807. Ohio, as a state, was just four years old. Columbus wouldn't be conceived of for another five years. In fact, the state capital at that time was almost 50 miles south, in the bustling little town of Chillicothe. There were no canals, no trains and no National Road. Travel from city to city was often made along small stagecoach paths.

Against this backdrop, a man whose name has been lost to history established a tavern five miles northeast of what would become downtown Columbus, near the west bank of Alum Creek. Known as Natchez-Under-the-Hill, the small business became a popular stop along the Cleveland – Lancaster – Marietta stagecoach route – later known as the Three C Highway.

According to oral history, it was at this inn that a pony rider stopped to change horses while riding north to alert citizens of the War of 1812. Natchez-Under-the-Hill, named for a more famous spot on the Mississippi River, became the center of social life for residents from miles around. Dances were regularly held here, with a three-piece string orchestra providing the musical backdrop.

Exactly when the old inn disappeared has been lost

The Valley Dale Ballroom has been a Central Ohio fixture for more than a century.

to time. Some say it was converted into today's Valley Dale Ballroom. Others insist Valley Dale was built from the ground up, but on the exact location of the earlier building. There's also a discrepancy as to when today's event space was built – 1918 or 1920, depending on whose account you believe. Historians seem to agree, however, that the original Valley Dale Ballroom burned to the ground just a few years later and was quickly rebuilt. For owner Jules Melancon, the new business was soon a major success. As early as 1923, a local bus company was offering nightly transportation to the Valley Dale from Broad and High.

The 1930s saw the arrival of the big band movement. Crooners and band leaders became the superstars of the day. And dance halls like Valley Dale began popping up all over the country – each trying to outdo the others by booking the biggest entertainers. Stars like Frank Sinatra, Bing Crosby,

Duke Ellington, Billie Holiday, Cab Calloway, Count Basie and dozens of others came to Valley Dale to perform for audiences of a thousand or more – either inside the luxurious ballroom or on a stage in the outdoor gardens.

Over the years, Valley Dale Ballroom has attracted entertainers as diverse as Rudy Vallee and Alice Cooper.

Earl Hood led the Valley Dale house band in those days. He once recalled some of the biggest engagements at the dance hall. He was quoted as saying, "The night Frank Sinatra sang with Tommy Dorsey was unforgettable. The girls were screaming and almost fainting; you couldn't hear yourself think." But even that paled in comparison to the night Guy Lombardo brought his Royal Canadians to town.

The Ed Hood Orchestra was the house band at Valley Dale from 1928 through 1950.

In the years before television, radio fueled the popularity of these and countless other stars. And Valley Dale was ready to take advantage of it. Melancon, the owner, built two radio booths – one on each side of the stage – from which emcees could introduce live talent. It wasn't unusual for CBS to split an occasional weeknight program between New York and Columbus, with a second, identical show three hours later for listeners on the West Coast.

Big band continued to rule the airwaves after World War II. But fewer of the orchestras were willing to travel to places like the Midwest, so local ones stepped in to fill the void. And then as Rock 'n' Roll cemented its hold on America, every local garage band in Central Ohio clamored for a gig at Valley Dale. High school dances, beauty pageants, weddings and private parties found their way into the ballroom, alongside the occasional appearance by local music groups like the Rick Brunetto Big Band, the Bruno Masdea Big Dance Band and the Bob Allen Trio.

Valley Dale received a one-million-dollar facelift in 2015.

More recently, Valley Dale suffered through management turnovers and a general lack of upkeep. The iconic dance hall was closed for much of 2015 while undergoing a one-million-dollar renovation by new owners Made from Scratch, a local catering company. The century-old building received a new roof, eight new chandeliers with L.E.D. lighting, remodeled restrooms and more.

Today, the old Valley Dale Ballroom looks better than ever – its walls filled with photos and tributes to the early 20th century stars who put it on the map. And today, a whole new generation of Columbus residents is discovering this hidden gem.

TripAdvisor Says So

I F YOU WERE asked to guess the Number One tourist attraction in Columbus, what would it be? German Village? The zoo? The new National Veterans Memorial and Museum? Chances are it would not be the Wagner-Hagans Auto Museum in Schumacher Place.

In 2018, the Wagner-Hagans Auto Museum on East Kossuth Street rose to the top of the list of favorite Columbus attractions on the popular TripAdvisor website.

But during the summer of 2018, something odd happened at TripAdvisor, the world's largest travel website. Of

121 listed attractions in Columbus, Ohio, the private, little car museum on Kossuth Street rose to the Number One spot – not necessarily the most-visited, but the favorite of many reviewers. Apparently, it has something to do with algorithms.

The museum, a former auto repair shop, is open by appointment only.

No one seemed more surprised than Steve Wagner, himself – co-owner, curator and tour guide at the auto museum, with its concrete-block walls and boarded-up windows. The only sign reads, "Open by Appointment" and lists a phone number.

Wagner, a full-time mortgage lender, began collecting old and unusual cars decades ago. He's quick to volunteer that he is not married, and thus can spend his money on anything he pleases, thank you. In 1988, Wagner met a kindred spirit in

Mark Hagans, a used car dealer and a collector, himself. The two became friends, and in 2008 opened their museum in a former car repair shop at 476 East Kossuth Street, just west of Parsons Avenue. Hagans contributed several of his antique Packards. Wagner finished filling the 41-thousand-square-foot building with more than a dozen of his old and unusual cars. By mutual decision, Wagner took on the role of tour leader.

A wall of auto tags shows off just a small portion of Wagner's extensive license plate collection.

The cars are in mint condition and look like they just came off a dealer's lot. There's the much-maligned 1958 Edsel, bright red; a navy blue 1956 Cadillac; and the baby blue 1958 Chrysler Imperial, complete with a pull-out record player that hides under the dash when not in use. There's even a 1979 AMC Pacer, often regarded as the worst passenger automobile ever created. And Wagner has an interesting story about every one of them.

In fact, it's Wagner's affable and easygoing personality that makes the place such a pleasure to tour. He truly enjoys showing people his cars ... and his license plates, too. Museum walls are covered with auto tags from around the world. He also has a plate from the year he was born (1949) from every state. But he's especially proud of his single-character Ohio license plates. He owns two, each of which has a single letter or numeral. Obviously, they're rare, and therefore both difficult and expensive to obtain.

Perhaps the most interesting plate in the collection is the 1943 Illinois tag. During World War II, most of the steel produced in the United States went into making weapons, vehicles and all manner of equipment for the war effort. The one from Illinois, which has the feel of cheap leather wrapped around cardboard, is made from soy beans. When Wagner adds that goats would occasionally eat them right off the bumpers, his relaxed expression gives you no clue as to whether he's telling the truth.

About 2014, a visiting couple asked Wagner if they

might mention his museum on TripAdvisor. And that's all it took. Soon, the co-owner's phone was ringing day and night with people asking to visit. That led to more happy tour-goers leaving high marks on the website. And in the summer of 2018, the Wagner-Hagans Auto Museum landed at the Number One spot on the popular internet website.

Steve Wagner estimates he's given as many as 300 free tours of his museum in a single year.

A few years ago, Wagner and Hagans decided to go their separate ways. Seems they had different visions for the museum. It was completely amicable, though, and now Hagans runs a Packard museum about 20 miles north of Columbus. His old partner highly recommends it. About the time Hagans moved out, marketing executive Jay Borman and his wife moved into a house near the Schumacher Place museum. And after a couple of years, Jay became Wagner's new partner. The name was changed to the Wagner-Jaybird Auto Museum. But no one could figure out how to change the name on TripAdvisor without deleting all the customer comments. So, Wagner-Hagans or Wagner-Jaybird, the owners will answer to either.

Hagans' Packards were replaced by Borman's antique military vehicles – jeeps, trucks, motorcycles and more, dating back to World War II. Like his predecessor, Borman seems content having Wagner conduct the tours. Evenings and weekends are the best times to schedule a visit. And, surprisingly, there is no admission charge. Wagner keeps a donation can near the front entrance, but he readily admits to having plenty of money and says he doesn't really need any more.

At a time when entertainment costs have risen to levels many families can't afford, it's nice to know there's a friendly man willing to show you his old cars and license plates and not ask you for a dime. Perhaps that Number One ranking shouldn't be a such surprise, after all.

VATICAN-OWNED

NOT MANY INSTITUTIONS can claim a direct link to the pope. And that's exactly what makes the Pontifical College Josephinum in Worthington unique. It is the only pontifical college outside Italy and the only seminary in the Western Hemisphere to report directly to the pope. "Pontifical" means it falls under the direct supervision of the Vatican.

John Joseph Jessing and two of the orphans he cared for. Jessing's seminary opened in 1888 as an outgrowth of his orphanage.

So, how did a small seminary in Ohio come to gain such an unusual status? It started with John Joseph Jessing, a German immigrant who dedicated his life to helping orphans. At the age of 34, Jessing entered the priesthood after studying at Mount Saint Mary's Seminary of the West, in Cincinnati.

In 1870, Jessing

was assigned to Pomeroy, Ohio, where he established St. Joseph's Orphanage and started a German-language Catholic newspaper to help cover the expenses. A few years later, Jessing received permission to move his orphanage and newspaper to Columbus, where he hoped to raise more money for his work through increased sales of his newspaper.

When two of his older orphans expressed an interest in joining the priesthood, Jessing put a notice in his paper, asking if there were any others. The response was good, and in 1888 the priest opened his Collegium Josephinum with an inaugural class of 23 students. Jessing wanted to make sure the seminary would continue after his death. And he wanted it to have importance on the national stage. So, he asked that the school be given to the Vatican.

Jessing's Collegium Josephinum opened in 1888 near downtown Columbus. In 1931 the school moved to its new campus in Worthington.

At the time, Pope Leo XIII was preparing the Roman Catholic Church for the 20th century, and he recognized the growing importance of the American continent for the purpose of spreading the Gospel. So, in 1892, he granted Jessing's request. The school would forever after be known as the Pontifical School Josephinum.

Jessing died in 1899, just a few months after watching his first class of priests graduate. In 1931, the Josephinum moved from East Main and 17th Street to its current, 100-acre campus in Worthington. John Joseph Jessing would be pleased to know that the seminary is still going strong and still occupies a unique place in the Catholic Church.

The Pontifical School Josephinum, in Worthington. The seminary moved from downtown Columbus to its current location in 1931.

The Walk O' Wonders

IT'S NO SECRET that shopping centers are having to get creative these days to compete with outlet malls and online shopping. They've added escape rooms, laser tag, trampoline parks, even skydiving simulators – all in the hope

Steve Skilken stands next to the 22-foot-tall Eiffel Tower replica that was once a part of the Walk O' Wonders. Steve's father, Joseph, owned the land that became the Great Western Shopping Center.

of luring the buying public to their retail stores. But there's no shopping center attraction that comes close to the one that drew huge crowds to the Great Western Shopping Center on West Broad Street back in the 1950s.

It was called the Walk O' Wonders, faithfully reproduced scale models of nine of the most famous tourist destinations in the world – all on display along a 700-foot walkway in the parking lot of the new, 53-store shopping center.

A 22-foot-tall Eiffel Tower; Niagara Falls, with flowing water and nearby buildings; the Taj Mahal, with a huge goldfish pool and fountains; the Parthenon and surrounding ruins atop the Acropolis. And beneath those Greek ruins – Carlsbad Caverns, viewed through small windows. Electric fans caused the miniature, hanging cave bats to gently sway in the breeze.

The Walk O' Wonders was the brainchild of pioneering shopping center developer Don Casto. Previously, Casto had built the Grandview Bank Block on Grandview Avenue, the first retail center in the country with integrated parking and Town & Country, believed by some to be the very first suburban shopping center. Casto, son Don Casto, Junior and business partner Joseph Skilken began planning the new shopping center at the same time other developers were starting Westland Mall, barely a mile away.

The Castos and Skilken, who owned the property, knew they needed something special to attract businesses and keep them from locating with the competition. Don Casto, Sr., is said to have floated the idea of the miniature reproductions during a party for potential shopping center tenants. Some say – only half-jokingly – that alcohol may have played a part in the suggestion. Regardless, the retailers seemed to love the idea.

It wasn't long before Skilken and the Castos became concerned that they had committed to more than they could produce. And in the end, it was noted that the Walk O' Wonders cost 165 thousand dollars to build, equaling the price of the shopping center, itself. By leap of faith, they pushed onward, choosing which "wonders" to build and hiring celebrated local artist and sculptor Ivan Pusecker to direct their construction.

The Niagara Falls replica featured an overlook that allowed visitors a close-up view of the intricate model. Photo courtesy Steve Skilken.

It was Pusecker's talent and attention to detail that

made the Walk so successful. He also hired a local sculptor who had once lived near the Leaning Tower of Pisa to recreate the iconic building, including exact replicas of all 118 columns. Pusecker installed a viewing platform atop the eight-foot-deep Grand Canyon to give people a better view of the river below. (Despite contemporary newspaper reports to the contrary, builders did not bury uranium ore among the canyon's peaks so visitors could test their Geiger counters.)

The Walk O' Wonders was introduced to the public on July 15th, 1956, one year after the surrounding stores had opened. Every dignitary in town was invited. Columbus Mayor Jack Sensenbrenner tossed a small barrel over Niagara Falls. A young Indian woman was flown to Columbus to stand beside the Taj Mahal. The crowd was ecstatic, marveling at the Sphinx and the Great Pyramids of Giza. Children threw coins in the Trevi Fountain, which was located in a corner of the parking lot, away from the rest of the attractions.

To say the Walk O' Wonders was a popular destination is an understatement. And in an age when Disneyland was brand new and trans-Atlantic air travel was still in its infancy, it also served as a popular educational tool. Schoolchildren on field trips arrived at the Great Western Shopping Center by the busload to learn about the world's great natural wonders and engineering feats.

But as awe-inspiring as they were, the individual "wonders" did not hold up well against the elements. The miniature Niagara Falls, with its complicated plumbing system,

The Taj Mahal model included working fountains and detailed landscaping. Photo courtesy Steve Skilken.

proved troublesome – especially when young mischief makers discovered how much fun it was to dump a box of soap powder into the swirling waters below.

The Walk O' Wonders lasted about a decade, with the last attraction, the Eiffel Tower, finally coming down in 1972. Today, it stands outside the home of Joseph Skilken's son, Steve, near Hoover Dam.

Great Western Shopping Center remained a viable shopping center – without the Walk O' Wonders – for the next few decades, until changing buying habits began to take their toll on retailers across the country. Today, its early competitor, Westland Mall, is empty. And the once-proud Great Western, with a dwindling occupancy, was placed on the auction block in 2017.

One has to wonder – among new attractions like ballerina and karate studios, the artisan pizza kitchens and babysitting services – if today's shopping centers might benefit from another Walk O' Wonders.

WAT'S IN A NAME?

T UCKED AWAY AMONG the modest homes and apartment complexes of the Berwyn East neighborhood on Columbus' east side is a sight certain to demand your attention – a brightly painted, intricately detailed Buddhist

The ornate Wat Lao Buddhamamakaram Buddhist temple in East Columbus was created by Laotian monks and temple volunteers. Photo by Andrew Livelsberger.

temple. In recent years, Lao Buddhist temples, or "wats," have sprung up across the United States to care for the spiritual needs of the country's many, small Laotian communities. Watlao Buddhamamakaram, on Bexvie Avenue just north of I-70, joined Central Ohio's growing number of Buddhist temples in 2009.

First, you notice the bright colors – reds, blues and yellows. Then you come face-to-face with a pair of three-headed "dragons," which appear to slither down the sides of the long staircase and walkway that lead to the building's main

The temple, built in 2009, serves a community of about 375 people – mostly Laotian immigrants. Photo by Andrew Livelsberger.

entrance. And then, the many small flourishes – some building details appearing as small "licks" of flame along the roofline.

The temple usually houses three or four monks at any one time and serves a congregation of about 375 people. Not all are Laotian, and the community welcomes visitors every day of the week. Most visits to the "wat" are made in the morning – usually about 10 a.m. That's when lay people from the surrounding Laotian community arrive to offer food to the resident monks. Monks have no personal belongings and depend on the generosity of the community they serve for their food and shelter.

If you go, you'll want to follow traditional Laotian etiquette. Whether you enter the wat or the nearby community center, wear conservative clothing. Remove your shoes before you enter. You'll be expected to sit on the floor and cross your legs. Never point your feet toward another person or an image of Buddha. That is considered highly offensive.

Remember these few rules and you'll be welcomed by some of the nicest, gentlest people you're ever likely to encounter. But don't expect to have a long conversation with any of the residents, as most have a very limited use of English.

WHISTLE WHILE YOU WORK

A S FAR AS factories go, it isn't much to look at – one large room at the back of a cinder-block building it shares with a company that makes spray-on truck bed liners. Some of the equipment is more than a century old. It employs fewer than a dozen people. It operates just one shift a day.

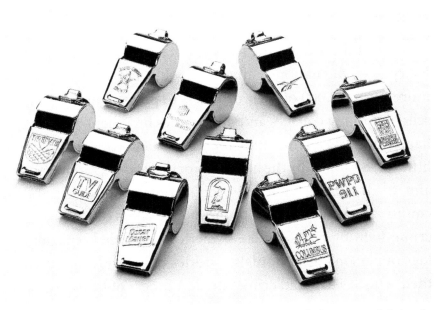

American Whistle Corporation offers personalized stamping with the customers' choice of logo or text.

But the dedicated people who work here produce something you won't find being manufactured anywhere else in the United States. Welcome to the American Whistle Corporation, which turns out more than a million metal whistles every year – solid brass whistles that are individually cut, stamped, bent, soldered, plated, smoothed and polished – all on the tiny, 4,000-square-foot factory floor.

There was a time when American Whistle catered mostly to sports teams, and that's still an important segment of their business. Using its 37-ton press, the company can produce whistles with stamped logos to match every sport and team imaginable. Since the early 1990s, the company has proudly produced specially engraved whistles for use by referees in the Super Bowl.

But these days, the sales emphasis has turned to safety. Every year, the nation's only metal whistle manufacturer sells more than 100,000 of their products to primary and secondary schools. Many colleges and universities buy them every fall, to hand out to their new students. Police departments buy these little "safety tools" by the hundreds of thousands, for themselves and to distribute to neighborhood organizations across the country. Lest anyone doubt the effectiveness of a whistle as a crime-fighting or safety tool, American Whistle keeps detailed logs of personal testimonials – stories of individuals who blew their whistles to avoid crimes or alert others of heart attacks or other emergencies.

So, why metal? And why brass? A metal whistle is louder than one made of plastic, which deadens the sound. Brass is a better amplifier than other metals and produces an excellent resonance – just like the brass musical instruments used by marching bands. These premium whistles are usually metal plated, too – with nickel, brass, bronze, sometimes even 24-karat gold.

A coil of brass from which metal American Whistles are stamped.

The type of whistle made in Columbus is known as a "pea whistle," for the little ball you'll find inside each one. The pea whistle was invented in 1879 and remains the most popular type. That little ball bounces around inside the whistle chamber when you blow, causing the variations in pitch, or "trilling." These days, American Whistle uses a proprietary, synthetic cork ball for better performance.

You'll learn these and more whistle facts if you take the factory tour. It's cheap (about $4), and at the end you'll get your own metal whistle to take home. The factory even has its own gift shop (actually more of a gift "counter"), where you'll find accessories like lanyards and rubber safety tips, along with souvenir t-shirts, mugs, magnets and more.

In the immortal words of Lauren Bacall, "You know how to whistle, don't you? Just put a made-in-Columbus metal whistle in your mouth and blow."

A workforce of fewer than a dozen people produces more than a million metal whistles each year.

A Worldwide Scam

The Hartman Hotel at Fourth and Main Streets as seen in 1901, just three years after it was built. Hartman and his wife spent most of their time in a large apartment on the second floor.

THE HARTMAN BUILDING at Fourth & Main is one of the last tangible connections to a Columbus millionaire whose medical quackery helped lead to the formation of the U.S. Food and Drug Administration.

Pennsylvania-born Samuel Hartman had a long and successful career as an itinerant medical doctor – traveling the country in the mid-19th century to help people who had problems with their ears or eyes. He also claimed to be a specialist in the treatment of catarrh – a build-up of mucus, usually in the sinus cavity. Hartman came to believe (or so he said) that catarrh could form around just about any organ in the body and was responsible for a wide range of illnesses. He began prescribing an elixir he had invented. He called it Peruna.

Dr. Samuel Hartman made millions of dollars from his fake medicines. His business practices also led to the formation of the U. S. Food and Drug Administration.

Hartman made up the name, sometimes spelling it "Pe-Ru-Na." He thought it would be easy to pronounce and easy to remember. Peruna was nothing more than water, alcohol, a touch of flavoring and a bit of burnt sugar for color. In fact, the alcohol content was almost 30 percent, which may be the reason so many "patients" said it made them feel better, at least temporarily. Wherever Hartman went to treat patients, he would have local pharmacists mix the elixir on their own. But the doctor became dissatisfied with the uniformity of the mixtures and finally decided to manufacture it, himself.

First, he made Peruna and a couple of other patent medicines in Osborn, Ohio, near Dayton. But in 1885, as business began to take off, he moved his operations to downtown Columbus. When a pharmacist in West Texas named Frederick Schumacher ordered an entire train car full of Peruna, Hartman knew he had found the man to help drive his business. Schumacher moved to Columbus, married Hartman's daughter Maribel and took the reins of Peruna's extensive newspaper advertising. Soon, the Peruna Drug Manufacturing Company was one of the largest "medical laboratories" in the country, producing what Hartman, himself, called "the purest, most prompt, and efficient medicine known to man."

A typical newspaper ad for Peruna. Ads generally consisted of fake testimonials from non-existent "patients."

By the turn of the century, Hartman was spending a million dollars a year on advertising – mostly in newspaper testimonials. Peruna became the top-selling elixir in the country. And it wasn't long before the doctor and his son-in-law became multi-millionaires.

The mass production of Peruna in the 1880s happened to coincide with the growing temperance movement, when states began passing their own prohibition laws. A "medicinal" tonic that was 28 percent alcohol became especially popular among those for whom liquor was unavailable. Reports of people getting drunk from Peruna became common. The federal government went so far as to ban the sale of Peruna and similar patent medicines to Native Americans, for fear of exacerbating a growing problem with alcoholism on reservations.

The Peruna plant took up most of a city block ... and continued growing. Several multi-story buildings went up, including a new, six-story headquarters along South Fourth Street, between Cherry and East Main, in 1898. Within three years, this building was converted to a luxury hotel to serve the wealthy patients at Hartman's "surgical hospital," next door – with access by way of a covered skywalk over Cherry Street.

Hartman also built one of the city's finest downtown theaters, the Hartman, which was demolished for a parking lot in 1971. He bought and operated a 4,000-acre farm on High Street, south of Columbus, which provided much of the city's milk needs. He even started his own bank to help him keep up with all his profits. Though Hartman and his wife owned a mansion on Town Street, they preferred to spend their winters in a large apartment on the third floor of the Hartman Hotel.

But in 1905, Hartman's empire began crumbling. An enterprising reporter for Collier's, a highly regarded weekly magazine, began writing a series of articles about medical fraud. Knowing that Peruna was little more than a means to become intoxicated, reporter Samuel Hopkins Adams approached Hartman about being interviewed. To Adams' surprise, Hartman agreed.

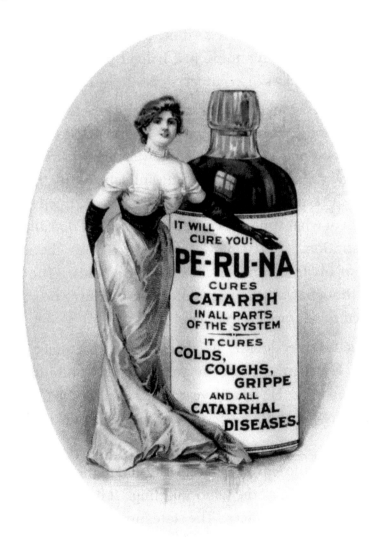

Hartman claimed that his elixir, containing almost 30% alcohol, could cure
just about anything that ailed a person.

Even more surprising was what Hartman told Adams. For reasons that were never understood, he readily admitted that Peruna did not cure anything. In fact, he said, there were no such things as cures. He said most ailments cleared up on their own, and that his tonic just helped people get through them with a little less discomfort.

Congress took notice of the Collier's articles – especially the interview with Samuel Hartman. A year later, they passed the Pure Food and Drug Act – the government's first attempt at consumer protection in the drug industry. This new law, signed by President Theodore Roosevelt, led directly to the formation of what would become known as the Food and Drug Administration. Hartman was forced to lower the alcohol content of his tonic and disclose its ingredients. The "new" Peruna, though, was still more potent than wine or beer, and it continued to sell moderately well.

As for the doctor, he died in his apartment at the Hartman Hotel in 1918 – one year before Prohibition took effect nationwide. He was 87 years old. The Peruna Company limped along for another 25 years or so, before finally folding in the 1940s.

In 1921, the Hartman Hotel was sold to the State of Ohio and became known as the Ohio Building. It housed a number of state agencies and offices. The state moved out in the 1970s, and the building fell into disrepair, leading a group of business people to buy it in 1998. Shops continued to operate on the first floor; and in 2005 the upper floors began being converted into condominiums. Meanwhile, Hartman's enormous farm continues to be operated by a family trust.

Today, few Columbus residents have even heard of Samuel Hartman or his luxury hotel or his famous "patent medicine," which played a large role in establishing this country's consumer protection laws.

WORKS CITED

Columbus Citizen-Journal

Columbus Dispatch

Columbus Dispatch Magazine

Columbus Monthly

This Week German Village

Columbus ALIVE

The History of the Great Southern Theater, Thesis by Marcia A. Siena, 1957

ThisWeek Community News

German Village Society Archives

Columbus City Directories

U. S. Patent Office

The Stark County Democrat

Columbus This Week

Business First

Roadside America

Clintonville Historical Society

The Lantern, The Ohio State University

The Age of a Glacial Erratic Located on the OSU Campus, Thesis by Robert L. Peters, 1971

Waverly Courier-Watchman

Colliers Weekly

Bottles and Extras – Collectors' Publication
American Heritage
Yale University EliScholar
Old Trails Museum, Winslow, Arizona
Ohio History Connection
New York Times
Columbus Department of Public Utilities
Ancestry.com
Ohio State Journal
Columbus Underground
Places of the Underground Railroad
TouringOhio.com
Columbus Neighborhoods

Printed in the USA
CPSIA information can be obtained
at www.ICGtesting.com
LVHW021309111223
766201LV00013B/969

9 781619 845664